THE BASICS OF THE HUMAN BODY

CORE CONCEPTS

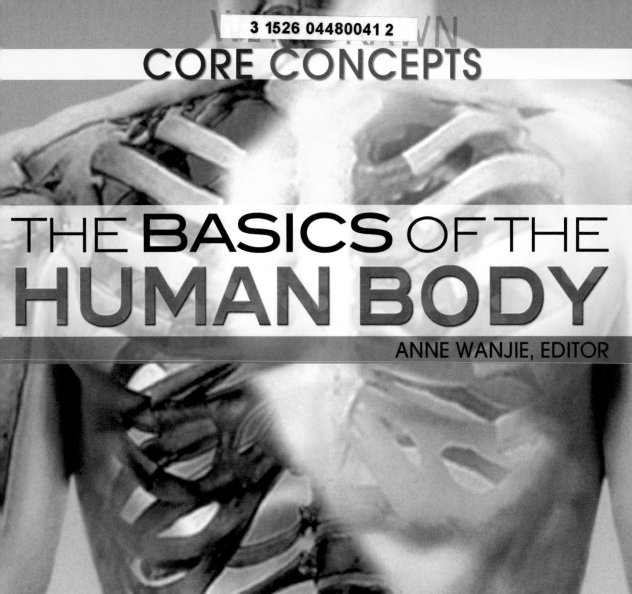

THE **BASICS** OF THE **HUMAN BODY**

ANNE WANJIE, EDITOR

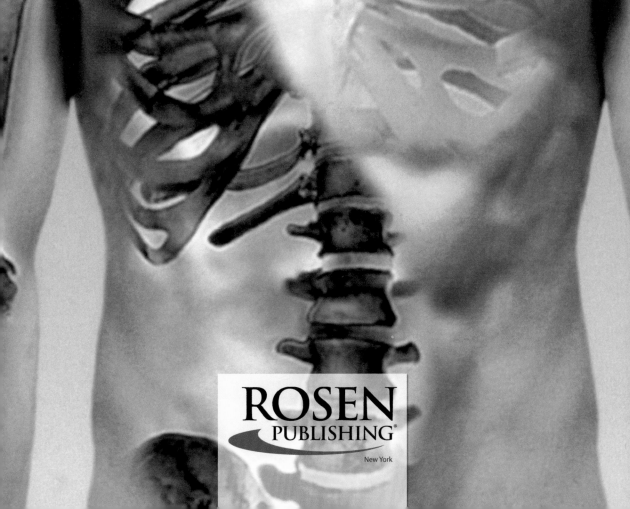

ROSEN
PUBLISHING®

New York

This edition published in 2014 by:

The Rosen Publishing Group, Inc.
29 East 21st Street
New York, NY 10010

Additional end matter copyright © 2014 by The Rosen Publishing Group, Inc.

Library of Congress Cataloging-in-Publication Data

Wanjie, Anne.
The basics of the human body/Anne Wanjie.—1st ed.—New York: Rosen, c2014
        p. cm.—(Core concepts)
Includes bibliographical references and index.
ISBN 978-1-4777-0555-1 (library binding)
1. Human body—Juvenile literature. 2. Human biology—Juvenile literature. I. Title.
QP37 .W36 2014
612

Manufactured in the United States of America

CPSIA Compliance Information: Batch #S13YA: For further information, contact Rosen Publishing, New York, New York, at 1-800-237-9932.

© 2004 Brown Bear Books Ltd.

CONTENTS

CHAPTER ONE

THE BODY'S ORGANS AND SYSTEMS

THE HUMAN BODY

ENDOCRINE SYSTEM
produces hormones (tiny "messenger" proteins) and includes the pituitary gland.

LUNGS
are the key organs in the respiratory system, which exchanges the waste gas carbon dioxide for the vital gas oxygen.

MUSCLES
in the muscular system contract or relax so the body can move.

URINARY SYSYTEM
expels fluid waste and includes the kidneys and bladder.

TENDONS
connect muscles to bones.

LYMPHATIC AND IMMUNE SYSTEMS
are made up of lymph vessels, lymph nodes, and white blood cells which protect the body from disease.

BRAIN
controls the nervous system, which includes nerves and the spinal cord.

SKIN, HAIR, AND NAILS
make up the integumentary system.

HEART AND BLOOD VESSELS
form the circulatory system, which carries gases and nutrients around the body.

STOMACH, LIVER, AND INTESTINES
belong to the digestive system, which breaks down food.

REPRODUCTIVE ORGANS
enable people to produce offspring.

SKELETAL SYSTEM
is made up of bones that protect the organs and support the body.

Your body is made up of interconnected groups of organs and tissues that keep you alive, healthy, and working correctly. They are called the body's systems.

The human body's systems begin to develop very early in life. An unborn baby starts off as just a single cell called a zygote. After the egg is fertilized by a sperm, it splits into two identical cells. These two cells each divide again to make four cells, and then they divide to make eight cells, and so on over and over again.

At first all the new cells are identical, but soon different kinds of

GREEK ANATOMY

Until the 16th century most of the Western world's knowledge of human anatomy (the structure of the body and its systems) was based on the writings of the physician Claudius Galen (130–201 CE). Galen was born in Greece but worked in Rome, where he tried to figure out how the human body works by studying the insides of dead apes and pigs. Many of Galen's books about anatomy and medicine became the main source of information for medical students for more than a thousand years.

cells start to appear. These cells form themselves into different types of tissues, which then develop into bone, muscle, and organs such as the heart and liver. The tissues and organs make up the basic parts of the body's systems. For example, organs such as the stomach and gut are part of the digestive system.

TWO TYPES OF SYSTEMS

There are 10 systems in the human body. Six of them are called the major systems—not because they are more important than the others but because they extend through the whole body. The major systems are the skeletal system, the muscular system, the circulatory system (the heart and blood

LEARNING FROM THE DEAD

The ancient Egyptians knew about the insides of the human body from the way they prepared their dead for burial, although their conclusions were not always correct. They removed the internal organs, stuffed the body with herbs and spices, and then soaked it in chemicals. This treatment mummified (preserved) the body by drying it so that it would not rot. The internal organs, sealed in separate jars of preserving spices, were placed in the tomb alongside the body.

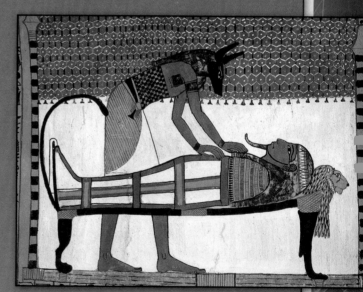

A mural depicts ancient Egyptian purification and burial practices as the body is prepared to be placed in its tomb.

AN. ÆT. XXVIII

THE HEART OF THE MATTER

Flemish anatomist Andreas Vesalius (1514–1564) was one of the first scientists to study human anatomy by examining people's bodies. In 1543 he published a book called *On the Fabric of the Human Body*. This book caused an outcry because it questioned the works of Galen, still the basis of medical science at that time. But it inspired researchers all over Europe to take a fresh interest in anatomy, and their work eventually led to the downfall of Galen's theories.

The last of Galen's ideas to bite the dust was about blood circulation. Galen

Andreas Vesalius published his findings about human anatomy in the 16th century.

vessels), the nervous system (the brain, spinal cord, and nerves), the integumentary system (the skin, hair, nails, and sweat glands), and the immune system (the cells in the blood that fight infection).

The other four systems—called the minor systems—are those inside the main body cavity, the chest and abdomen. The digestive system includes the

HOMEOSTASIS

As well as doing their own jobs, systems work together to control the physical and chemical conditions inside the body. This process, called homeostasis, includes keeping the body at the correct temperature, around 98.6°F (37.0°C). Sweating cools the body, and shivering is a warming mechanism. Other organs involved include the liver and pancreas, which control the concentration of sugar in the blood, and the kidneys, which control the body's water and salt content.

thought that blood was produced by the liver and pumped around the body by the opening and closing of the blood vessels (the arteries and veins). The heart was where the blood mixed with air from the lungs. Until the 17th century most physicians accepted this theory. Then in 1628 the English physician William Harvey (1578–1657) published his discovery that the heart pumps blood out through the arteries, and the blood returns to the heart through the veins.

The English physician William Harvey explains the circulation of blood to King Charles I in the 17th century.

mouth, stomach, liver, and intestines. It converts food into energy and nutrients such as amino acids and sugars. The main part of the respiratory system is the lungs, which absorb oxygen from the air when you breathe in and expel carbon dioxide gas when you breathe out. The excretory system includes the kidneys; the reproductive system includes the reproductive organs; and the endocrine system produces hormones (chemicals that help control all the other systems). Some organs are part of more than one of the body's systems. The pancreas, for example, is part of the digestive and endocrine systems.

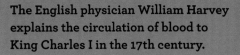

SECRETS OF THE STOMACH

In 1822 a French Canadian named Alexis St. Martin was accidentally shot in the side, and the U.S. Army surgeon William Beaumont (1785–1853) treated him. The wound healed, but it left St. Martin with a permanent hole in his side that connected directly to his stomach. Beaumont realized that this was a chance to study how the stomach digests food. He tied pieces of meat, bread, and cabbage to the ends of silk strings and put them into St. Martin's stomach. A few hours later he pulled them out to see what had happened to them. In 1833 Beaumont published a description of how digestion works in the stomach.

CHAPTER TWO

THE DIGESTIVE SYSTEM

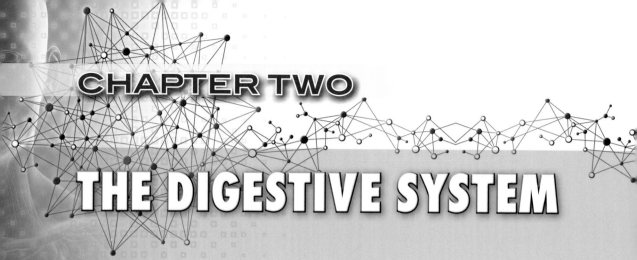

A healthy diet contains just a small amount of fat and sugar. It should also have plenty of dairy products, proteins such as meat and fish, vegetables and fruits, and carbohydrates such as bread and cereals.

SUGARS AND FATS

DAIRY

MEAT

VEGETABLES

FRUIT

CARBOHYDRATES

During digestion the body breaks down food into tiny particles that can dissolve in the blood. The particles are absorbed and carried to the body tissues. Excretion is the process by which the body gets rid of waste products after digestion.

Your body can use the food you eat only when the food is broken down into small, simple units, or molecules. Most food is composed of long chains of molecules. The digestive system has to break the links in the chains. This process reduces the large molecules to smaller ones, which are carried by the blood to the body's cells. The cells use them as fuel or reassemble them into new chains, forming the building blocks for new tissues. The chemical reactions inside the cells produce lots of waste products, which the blood carries away. Wastes are destroyed and removed from the body by organs in the excretory system, such as the kidneys, and by the liver.

A HEALTHY DIET

To stay healthy, the human body needs a continual supply of food to provide energy and chemical building blocks for growing new tissues and repairing damaged ones. There are three main types of food that you need to eat—proteins, carbohydrates, and fats. You also need to take in water, fiber, and small amounts of important substances called vitamins and minerals.

Proteins build muscles and create a vast range of complex chemicals inside the body's cells. They come from foods such as meat, cheese, fish, eggs, beans, and nuts. During digestion they break down into tiny molecules called amino acids, which dissolve in the blood and are carried around the body to where they are needed.

A well-balanced diet contains all the important food types. This is essential if you are to grow properly and have enough energy and strength for working and playing.

Carbohydrates provide a quick energy source. Complex carbohydrates, such as starch, come from foods such as rice and potatoes. Simple carbohydrates, or sugars, come from sweet foods and fruit juices. During digestion carbohydrates are broken down into molecules called monosaccharides. Body cells use carbohydrates to fuel the chemical reactions within the cells. If you eat more

DIETARY FIBER

Not everything you eat is digested. Dietary fiber, or roughage, is the name for all sorts of tough plant materials that the body cannot digest. Although your body does not digest fiber, it is an important part of your diet. It absorbs water and so adds bulk to food. That helps the digestive system push the food along the digestive tract. If you do not have enough fiber in your food, you might get disorders of the digestive system such as constipation or diarrhea.

This boy is suffering from a disease called rickets. It is caused by having too little vitamin D in the diet. Vitamin D helps the body take up calcium from food. Calcium makes bones healthy and strong. Many children with rickets have soft bones, which makes their legs bow outward.

carbohydrates than you need, the leftovers are turned into fat for storage.

Foods such as butter, oil, cheese, and chocolate are rich in fats. Fats contain twice as much energy per ounce as carbohydrates do, and so they provide a valuable long-term supply of energy for the body. They are also needed for making essential substances, including chemicals called hormones, which control processes in the body, and the molecules that form cell membranes. During digestion fats are broken down into particles called fatty acids, monoglycerides, and glycerol. Fats can also be used as a valuable supply of energy for the body.

Vitamins and minerals are important for keeping you healthy, but only very small amounts of most are required. Vitamins are a group of complex organic (carbon-containing) substances that play a key role in certain chemical reactions in the body. Vitamin A, for example, is essential for the normal growth of bones and teeth. It is also important for vision and helps you see in the dark.

Minerals are simple, inorganic compounds (ones that do not contain carbon) such as sodium and iron. Minerals

The human digestive system. The sections of the small intestine absorb food and further break down the food. The large intestine is mainly important for retrieving water from the remnants of the food.

also play important roles in body chemistry. Iron, for example, is needed to make hemoglobin, a chemical that binds to oxygen and is carried through the body by red blood cells.

BREAKING IT DOWN

Food is detected and analyzed by sense organs before and after it enters the mouth. There the food is chewed, and saliva begins to break it down. The food then passes through a long tube, called the digestive tract. In this tract chemicals called enzymes attack the food and break it down further. The remains of food that have not been digested finally leave the body through an opening called the anus.

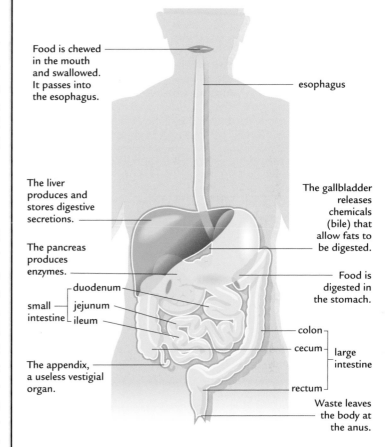

HUMAN DIGESTIVE SYSTEM

Food is chewed in the mouth and swallowed. It passes into the esophagus.

esophagus

The liver produces and stores digestive secretions.

The gallbladder releases chemicals (bile) that allow fats to be digested.

The pancreas produces enzymes.

Food is digested in the stomach.

small intestine — duodenum / jejunum / ileum

The appendix, a useless vestigial organ.

colon
cecum — large intestine
rectum

Waste leaves the body at the anus.

ENZYMES

Enzymes are proteins that speed up chemical reactions in the body. Cells contain thousands of different types of enzymes, each of which controls a particular reaction.

Digestive enzymes work outside cells, inside the organs of the digestive system. They speed up a chemical reaction called hydrolysis, in which water molecules attack chain molecules and break apart the links. Digestive enzymes are produced in the mouth, stomach, small intestine, and pancreas. Examples of digestive enzymes are the proteases, which break down proteins into amino acids.

CHEWING AND SWALLOWING

The process of digestion begins before you even eat anything. The sight and smell of food trigger the release of a slimy fluid called saliva, which moistens the food once it is in the mouth, making it easier to chew and swallow. The saliva also contains an enzyme that begins to break down a type of carbohydrate in the food called starch.

The powerful muscles of the jaw work together with the teeth to cut and mash the food until it is soft and moist enough to swallow. Taste buds on the tongue detect the four main tastes in food—salty, bitter, sweet, and acidic. Gases released by the warm food travel into the nose, where their smell contributes to the flavor. When you swallow your food, it travels down a tube called the esophagus to the stomach. The food does not simply fall into the stomach. It is pushed along the esophagus by waves of muscular squeezing (contraction) called peristalsis.

TEETH

People have 32 teeth, of which there are four different types: Incisors at the front for cutting, canines for piercing, and premolars and molars at the back for cutting and grinding. The white, visible part of a tooth is called the crown. It is covered with a substance called enamel, which is the hardest material in the human body. Under the enamel is a hard layer of dentine, and under it is the pulp cavity, which contains blood vessels and nerves. Each tooth is anchored into the jawbone by roots.

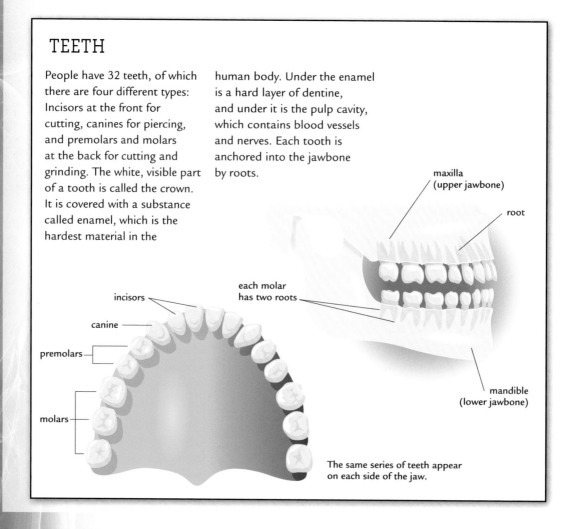

maxilla (upper jawbone)

root

incisors

each molar has two roots

canine

premolars

molars

mandible (lower jawbone)

The same series of teeth appear on each side of the jaw.

HOW SALIVA WORKS

You can learn the effects of enzymes for yourself by chewing some food. Put a piece of bread in your mouth, and chew it for 30 seconds. As the bread mixes with your saliva, it will start to taste sweeter. That happens because an enzyme called salivary amylase breaks down the carbohydrate starch into a sugar called maltose.

THE STOMACH AT WORK

The stomach is a stretchy muscular bag that expands as it fills up. Food spends up to four hours in the stomach being churned around by contractions of the muscles in the stomach wall. The lining of the stomach produces a digestive liquid called gastric

PERISTALSIS

The walls of the digestive system are made up of two layers of smooth muscle. One layer is arranged lengthways, and the other is arranged in rings. These muscles contract in a rhythmic way, causing the food to be pushed slowly along the digestive system. This action, called peristalsis, causes some of the gurgling noises and movements you can sometimes feel in your belly.

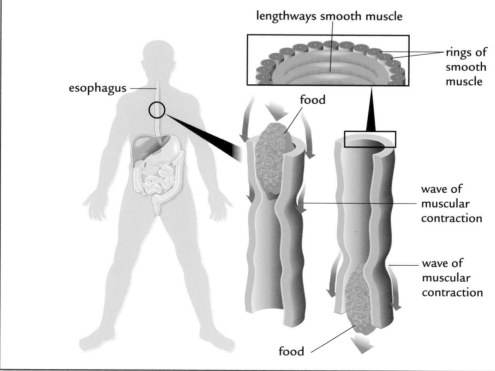

lengthways smooth muscle

rings of smooth muscle

esophagus

food

wave of muscular contraction

wave of muscular contraction

food

EMULSIFICATION

Pour a little vegetable oil into two glasses of warm water. Add soap liquid to one glass, then stir both of them quickly for around 10 seconds. The mixture containing soap liquid will form a milky fluid, but the other mixture will slowly separate back into layers of water and oil.

Fats and oils do not mix with water easily. They separate out as globules, which makes them difficult to digest. In the small intestine bile breaks down these globules by emulsifying them—it turns them into thousands of much tinier droplets. Soap liquid works in the same way bile does.

juice. It contains an enzyme called pepsin, which breaks down proteins in food, as well as hydrochloric acid, which kills germs and helps pepsin work by attacking proteins.

The stomach reduces the food to a creamy liquid, and contractions then squirt the fluid out of an opening called the pyloric sphincter into the first part of the small intestine, called the duodenum. Sphincters are rings of muscle that can open and close.

The bile duct wall, magnified many times. This duct takes bile to the small intestine from the gallblader.

THE SMALL INTESTINE'S BIG JOB

Most digestion takes place in the small intestine. In the duodenum food from the stomach mixes with two digestive juices—bile from the liver and pancreatic juice from the pancreas. Bile helps the digestion of fats by making larger droplets of liquid fat break down into microscopic droplets. This process is called emulsification. Bile is stored in a small sac called the gallbladder. Pancreatic juice contains many enzymes that digest proteins, carbohydrates, and fats. These enzymes continue working throughout the small intestine.

As a meal travels along the small intestine, most of the food within it is digested into small molecules. These molecules then pass across the lining

WHY DO DIGESTIVE SYSTEMS NOT DIGEST THEMSELVES?

The lining of the stomach and intestines would be digested if it were not well protected. Glands within it produce a thick fluid called mucus that protects the lining and makes it slippery, helping food move along. Even so, the walls of the digestive system suffer a lot of wear and tear, so they have to grow a new lining continually, just as skin does. Dead cells rub off the top of the lining and are carried away and digested.

of the intestine and enter the bloodstream to be carried away to the body's cells. The small intestine's lining has many fingerlike folds called villi (sing. villus) over its surface. They are covered by even tinier projections called microvilli. Inside each villus is a network of blood vessels (capillaries) with very thin walls, which pick up small molecules from digested food.

WASTE PRODUCTS AND THE LARGE INTESTINE

Undigested food enters the large intestine, which absorbs water and leaves behind a semisolid material. Harmless bacteria feed on this waste matter. They break down some of the fiber, releasing sugar and some vitamins, which are then absorbed by the body. The bacteria also produce hydrogen, methane, and carbon dioxide gas, which can build up and cause wind.

Waste matter spends up to two days in the large intestine. It collects as a material called feces in a part of the digestive tract called the rectum. The feces are pushed out by muscles in the rectum.

THE "CHEMICAL FACTORY"

The bloodstream carries digested food away from the intestines and to an organ called the liver. The liver works like a chemical factory. It carries out hundreds of tasks that keep the concentrations of sugar, amino acids, and various other chemicals in the blood just right. Excess

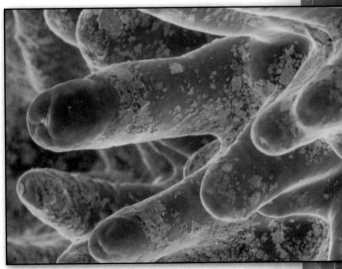

Fingerlike folds called villi cover the lining of the small intestine. The villi make the surface area much bigger than it would otherwise be, so there is a large area over which food molecules can be absorbed.

THE LIVER

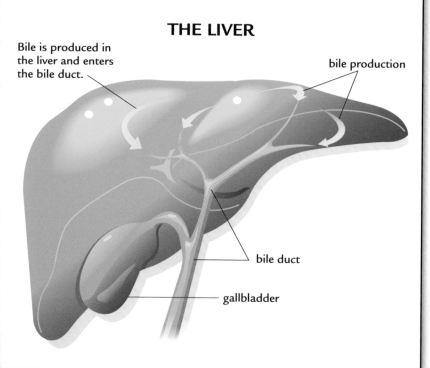

Bile is produced in the liver and enters the bile duct.

bile production

bile duct

gallbladder

food and iron are removed and stored in the liver for later. A sugar called glucose is turned into a carbohydrate called glycogen, which can be quickly broken down and released again as glucose when it is needed in the body.

The liver also destroys poisons, such as alcohol, that enter the body with food. The liver manufactures vitamin A, breaks down worn-out blood cells, and creates bile.

FILTERING BLOOD

The kidneys are two organs in the lower back shaped like large beans. They are the main organs of excretion. They continually filter the blood, removing water and chemical wastes. Each kidney contains about one million individual tubes called nephrons.

Blood enters each nephron through a knot

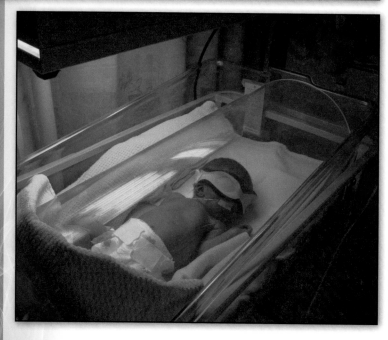

A newborn baby receives phototherapy to treat jaundice, a problem that occurs when the liver makes too much bile.

A KIDNEY

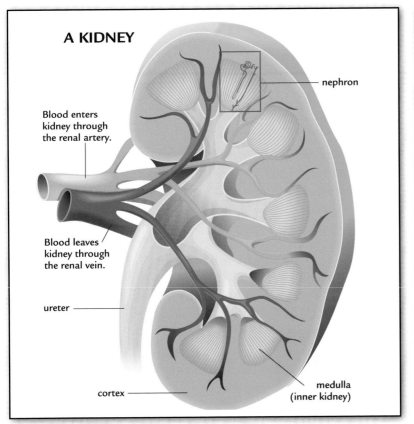

nephron

Blood enters kidney through the renal artery.

Blood leaves kidney through the renal vein.

ureter

cortex

medulla (inner kidney)

NEPHRON

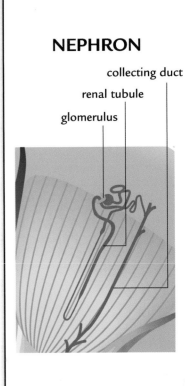

collecting duct

renal tubule

glomerulus

of tiny blood vessels called a glomerulus. The glomerulus works just like a sieve. It allows water and other small molecules (including salts, sugars, and chemical wastes such as urea) to leave the blood and enter a long, looped tube called a renal tubule. The renal tubule is surrounded by even more tiny blood vessels. As the filtered blood moves through the renal tubule, sugars and salts are taken back into the blood, along with water. At the same time, waste molecules are left in the nephron or secreted into it.

More than 99 percent of the fluid entering the nephron from the blood is taken back into the body. The rest drains out of the nephrons through collecting ducts. It leaves the kidneys and passes along tubes called ureters to collect in the bladder. At this point the fluid is called urine. When the bladder fills up, it sends a nerve signal to the brain, causing the feeling of wanting to urinate (pass water).

CHAPTER THREE

THE CIRCULATORY SYSTEM

The circulatory system is all the tubes and channels (blood vessels) through which blood flows and the heart, which pumps blood around the body.

A surgeon holds a human heart, which will be transplanted into a patient whose own heart is not working properly. During the operation the patient is connected to a heart bypass machine, which adds oxygen to the blood and pumps it around the body while the new heart is attached.

The blood vessel system is like a many-branched vine. The largest blood vessels enter and leave the heart. They get smaller and smaller as they branch out to reach all the body cells. The blood and circulatory system are essential in transporting oxygen, nutrients, and waste materials around the body. The system also helps coordinate all the other body systems. The blood is also part of the immune (defense) system. It contains white blood cells that help fight infection by microorganisms.

THE CIRCULATORY SYSTEM'S ENGINE

Most of the time you are not aware of your heart. However, when you exercise or when you are frightened or angry, you can feel it beating powerfully and sense the blood pounding in your head. The heart is the engine of the circulatory system, which supplies all parts of your body with blood.

The heart is a pump located in the center of your chest. It has four hollow chambers; the top two are called atria (singular, atrium), and the two at the bottom are called ventricles. The heart's structure and function are so unique that many of its workings are still not well understood.

The tissue that makes up the heart is called cardiac muscle. Like the smooth muscle that surrounds hollow organs, such as the intestines, cardiac muscle can squeeze (contract) involuntarily—you do not have to "tell" your heart muscle to work; it does it automatically. Yet, like the muscles attached to your bones (skeletal muscles), heart muscle is striated (made of long fibers). So, cardiac muscle is a cross between smooth muscle and skeletal muscle.

Cardiac muscle also has unique connections between its cells that help all the heart's muscle cells contract rapidly and at the same time.

On average, the adult heart beats around 72 times per minute. Around 3 fluid ounces (80ml) of blood are pumped into the main artery with each beat, so the heart usually pumps up to 1½ gallons (7 liters) of blood per minute. During strenuous

THE HUMAN HEART

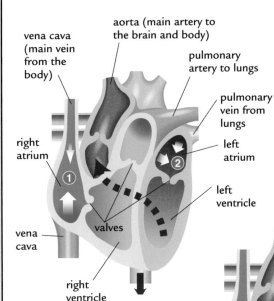

aorta (main artery to the brain and body)

vena cava (main vein from the body)

pulmonary artery to lungs

pulmonary vein from lungs

right atrium

left atrium

left ventricle

vena cava

valves

right ventricle

1. Oxygen-poor blood from the body enters the right atrium.

2. Oxygen-rich blood from the lungs enters the left atrium.

3–4. The atria contract to pump the blood into the ventricles through open heart valves.

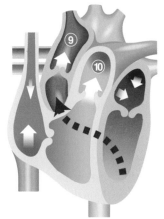

5–6. At the same time, the muscular walls of the ventricles relax to help blood enter.

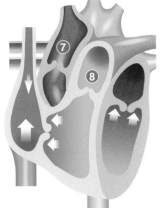

7–8. Valves open in the aorta and pulmonary artery, which goes to the lungs. Valves between the atria and ventricles close to keep blood flowing in the right direction.

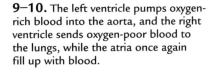

9–10. The left ventricle pumps oxygen-rich blood into the aorta, and the right ventricle sends oxygen-poor blood to the lungs, while the atria once again fill up with blood.

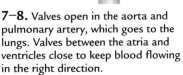

LISTENING TO YOUR HEARTBEAT

A stethoscope is an instrument used to listen to the heartbeat. In 1819 the French physician René Laënnec (1781–1826) made the first stethoscope out of a hollow wooden tube 1 inch (2.5cm) wide and 10 inches (25cm) long.

You can use a cardboard tube from the inside of a roll of paper towels to make a stethoscope. Work with a partner. Put one end of the tube high in the center of your partner's chest. Put your ear against the other end. Do you hear the "lubb-dubb" of the heartbeat? Count the number of heartbeats you hear in 30 seconds. Multiply by 2 to get the number of beats in 1 minute. That is your partner's heartbeat rate.

Listen carefully and count the number of heartbeats you can hear for a given length of time. A 12-year-old's heart usually beats around 85 times every minute, but this rate is more than doubled after strenuous exercise.

exercise such as running, that can rise to 6 gallons (27 liters) per minute in an average adult.

REGULATING THE HEART

Perhaps the most amazing feature of the heart is that it can control some of its own actions without any outside regulation, even from the brain. Tiny electrical impulses or bursts regulate the pumping of various parts of the heart. These impulses come from areas within the heart called nodes.

The sinoatrial (or SA) node is located on the wall of the right atrium. The impules sent from the SA node regulate the heartbeat. So the SA node is called the heart's pacemaker. Another node, called the atrioventricular (AV) node, slows the SA node impulses enough to allow the atria to finish contracting before the ventricles begin contracting. The impulses are sent rapidly to cardiac cells in the ventricles through cardiac muscle strands called Purkinje fibers.

People with a slow or irregular heartbeat can have a pacemaker put in their chest to control the beat.

The rhythmic contraction of heart muscles produces the "lubb-dubb" sound of the heartbeat. The "lubb" sound is when the atria have finished contracting, the atrial valves close, and the ventricles begin to contract. The

CHECKING YOUR PULSE

To check how fast your heart is beating, ask a partner to put two fingers on your wrist artery to feel your pulse. It is on the inside of your wrist. Use a stopwatch to count the number of pulses in 15 seconds. First, take your pulse when you are sitting and resting. Then, run for two minutes. Immediately after, take your pulse for 15 seconds. Multiply each number by 4 to get the number of pulses per minute. How much faster was your heart beating after you ran than when you were resting?

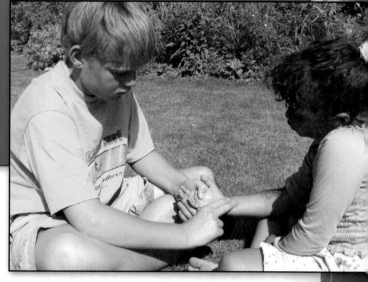

"dubb" sound occurs when the ventricles have pumped out blood, and the valves between the ventricles and the arteries close.

PUMPING BLOOD

Blood enters both atria at almost the same time from large blood vessels. They are the vena cavae, which carry oxygen-poor, or deoxygenated, blood from the body, and the pulmonary blood vessels, which carry oxygen-rich, or oxygenated, blood from the lungs back to the heart. Oxygen-poor blood enters the right atrium. Oxygen-rich blood from the lungs enters the left atrium.

The atria contract to pump the blood into the ventricles. When blood enters the atria, the ventricles are empty.

The thick, muscular walls of the ventricles relax, increasing their volume and pulling in blood through the atria from the veins. The atria then contract to pump the ventricles full of blood. Both ventricles then contract forcefully. The right ventricle pumps blood into arteries that carry it to the lungs to pick up oxygen. At the same time, the left ventricle pumps its oxygen-rich blood into the aorta—a large blood vessel that channels the blood to the brain and the rest of the body.

Valves between the heart chambers keep the blood flowing in the correct direction. The valve between the right atrium and ventricle is called the tricuspid valve. After the right atrium pumps blood into the right ventricle, the tricuspid valve closes. That stops the blood from flowing back into the atrium. The bicuspid, or mitral, valve does the same for the left atrium. The veins also have one-way valves

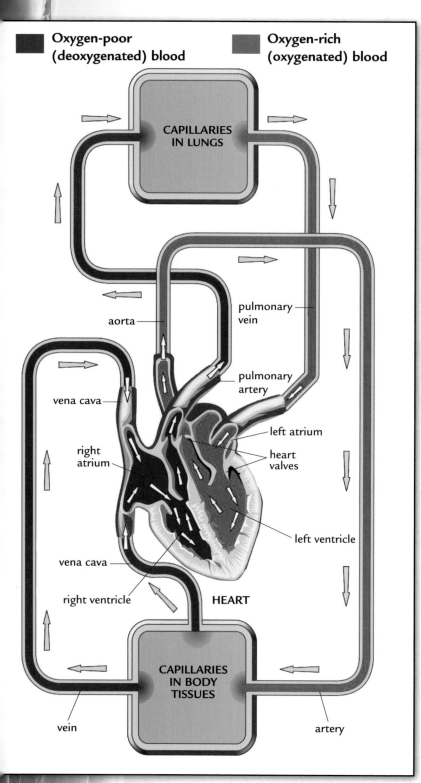

Oxygen-poor (deoxygenated) blood

Oxygen-rich (oxygenated) blood

CAPILLARIES IN LUNGS

pulmonary vein

aorta

pulmonary artery

vena cava

left atrium

right atrium

heart valves

left ventricle

vena cava

right ventricle

HEART

CAPILLARIES IN BODY TISSUES

vein

artery

Deoxygenated blood from the body goes to the right side of the heart. It is pumped to the lungs, where it offloads carbon dioxide and picks up oxygen. Oxygenated blood goes to the left side of the heart and is pumped around the body.

that allow blood to flow only toward the heart.

CARRYING BLOOD THROUGHOUT THE BODY

Blood vessels carry blood to nearly all the cells in the body. The aorta and other blood vessels attached directly to the heart are the body's largest blood vessels. The next largest are the major arteries, which branch into various parts of the body. Smaller blood vessels, called arterioles, branch off the arteries and get smaller and smaller, eventually forming a web of minute tubes that carry blood to every body cell. These smallest blood vessels are called capillaries, which are tubes with walls only one cell thick. A mass of capillaries in a piece of tissue is called a capillary bed.

HEART TRANSPLANTS

Some people with diseased hearts can be saved by transplanting a healthy heart into their body. There are not enough human hearts available, however. This has led surgeons to experiment with implanting baboon hearts into people. Many people are worried by such procedures; what if baboon viruses or other diseases are passed on to humans? Some people believe that transplanting organs from one species to another raises questions about what it means to be human. Are you still human if one of your vital organs is nonhuman? Others suggest that breeding animals to kill them for their organs is wrong. Supporters say that such experiments may save many lives.

Oxygen in the blood moves from the capillaries into the cells. In return the cells release carbon dioxide as waste into the capillaries. This process, called gas exchange, occurs at the capillary bed. The capillaries that receive carbon dioxide are the beginning of the system of veins that carries oxygen-poor blood back to the heart. Like the arteries, as veins approach the heart, they become larger. The vena cavae (singular, vena cava) are the largest veins. Veins are lined with one-way flap valves that keep the blood moving toward the heart, which is why blood does not gather in your feet.

The smooth muscles of the arteries near where they join with the capillaries expand or contract to regulate blood flow to different areas of the body. After you eat, arterioles carrying blood to the capillary beds of the stomach and intestines open to allow more blood to flow to the digestive tract. Arterioles in the arms and legs may contract and restrict blood flow during digestion. When it is hot

A capillary bed (1)—the site of gas exchange in the body's tissues—lies between a vein (2) and an artery (3). The arteries and arterioles (small arteries, 4) bring oxygenated blood to the capillary bed from the heart, while the venules (small veins, 5) and veins take deoxygenated blood back to the heart.

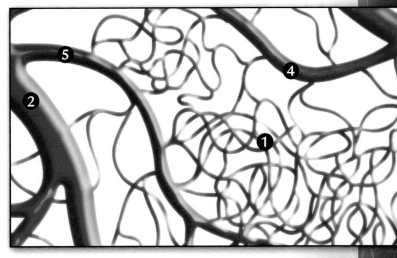

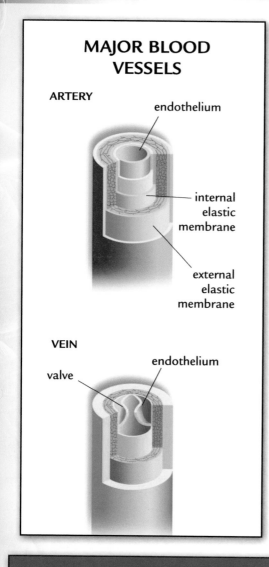

MAJOR BLOOD VESSELS

ARTERY

endothelium

internal elastic membrane

external elastic membrane

VEIN

endothelium

valve

Arteries receive blood from the heart. They have elastic fibers so they can withstand high pressures. Veins return blood to the heart. Some have valves to stop backflow.

outside, you may look "flushed" because arterioles near the skin surface open to allow more blood to flow to your skin, cooling it. When it is cold, you often look "drawn" because arterioles in the skin contract to limit blood flow and heat loss.

BLOOD CELLS

The blood carries oxygen and nutrients to all body cells and removes wastes from them. There are many types of blood cells, each with a distinct job to do. The clear liquid that carries all the blood cells is called plasma. There is about 1 gallon (5 liters) of blood in an adult's body. Red blood cells contain a substance called hemoglobin, which transports oxygen. Around 45 percent of blood consists of red blood cells. They are constantly produced in a tissue called bone marrow in the bones. An adult has around 25 trillion disk-shaped red blood cells in the blood.

HEART DISEASE

Heart disease is one of the leading causes of death in the United States. One major cause of heart disease is atherosclerosis. This condition is the accumulation in the arteries of fatty deposits rich in cholesterol. Fatty meat is by far the food that contributes most to atherosclerosis.

Some people have suggested that the government put a tax on meat to discourage people from eating it. Like the tax on tobacco, this fee could improve the health of millions of Americans and encourage them to eat more healthful whole grains instead of animal fat. What do you think of this suggestion?

TYPES OF WHITE BLOOD CELLS

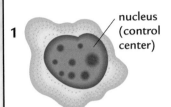
1
nucleus (control center)

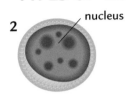
2
nucleus

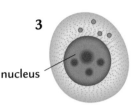
3
nucleus

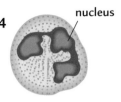
4
nucleus

Macrophages (1) engulf and destroy microorganisms. Lymphocytes, T or B cells (2), produce antibodies and kill infected cells. Natural killer cells (3) attack virus-infected or cancerous body cells. Neutrophils (4) destroy bacteria at the site of infection.

White blood cells protect against infection and disease. Each type of cell has a certain job to do. Most white cells in the body are neutrophils.

White blood cells, also made in the bone marrow, are part of your immune system. They include macrophages, T cells, B cells, natural killer cells, and neutrophils. Platelets are fragments of blood cells that are important in blood clotting. They stick together to form a fine mesh of fibers, which traps more blood cells. This process results in a clot that seals an injury or wound.

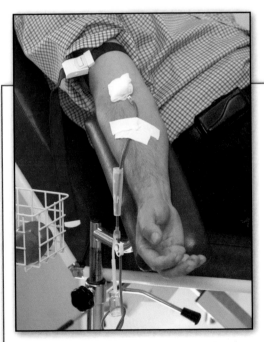

A needle has been inserted into a blood vessel in the donor's arm to take blood.

DONATING BLOOD

Victims of car accidents, people undergoing surgery, and those with certain diseases such as hemophilia (a blood-clotting disorder) often need to receive blood donated by others. Each year about 4 million Americans receive donated blood. A donor's blood is tested to make sure it is healthy. Then about 1 pint (0.5l) of blood is taken from the large vein in the donor's arm. In many cases the donated blood is then separated into its component parts, such as plasma, platelets, and so on. Different patients get just the blood components they need.

CHAPTER FOUR

THE RESPIRATORY SYSTEM

Breathing involves the movement of gases between the body and its environment. Biologists call this gas exchange. The organs that carry out this process make up the respiratory system.

Imagine a little girl who does not get what she wants. She may threaten to "hold her breath until she's blue." After one attempt to carry out this threat, most children are smart enough not to

For people it is impossible to breathe underwater. Divers must use a tank containing oxygen gas as well as other gases to breathe there.

UNDERSTANDING DIFFUSION

Imagine two types of molecules, O and C, separated by a membrane. The concentration of Os is greater on the left, so they diffuse to the right, where there are fewer Os. The concentration of Cs is greater on the right, so they diffuse across the membrane to the left, where there are fewer Cs. In time this diffusion will lead to both sides having equal concentrations of Os and Cs.

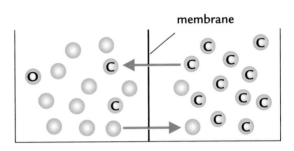

try again. But why can't the girl hold her breath for as long as she wants?

Every cell in your body needs a gas called oxygen to function. Breathing helps deliver this gas. It also takes away another gas, carbon dioxide, that is one of the waste products of a cell's functions. The little girl cannot hold her breath until she dies. Breathing is so important that it is controlled by the body's autonomic nervous system. This system regulates crucial body functions automatically in a way that is beyond our conscious control.

MOLECULES ON THE MOVE

Imagine a liquid in a jar separated into two halves by a membrane. One of the halves contains lots of dissolved salt; the other half has just a touch of salt.

WATCH DIFFUSION

Use an eyedropper to slowly add a few drops of food coloring to cold water in a clear container, and watch the drops diffuse. Add different colors, and observe the color of the water after 5 minutes and then after 10 minutes. You will see that the colors gradually blend as the food coloring particles diffuse into the water. Eventually the water will become a uniform color.

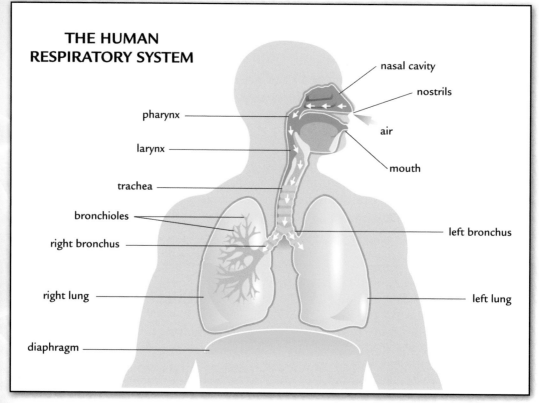

THE HUMAN RESPIRATORY SYSTEM

nasal cavity

nostrils

pharynx

air

larynx

mouth

trachea

bronchioles

left bronchus

right bronchus

right lung

left lung

diaphragm

The human respiratory system. The white arrows show the movement of air into the lungs.

After a time the salt concentrations in each half will become equal. That is because molecules (small particles) move from places where their concentration is high to places where their concentration is low. This movement of molecules is called diffusion.

Oxygen is needed to break down the fuels such as glucose that power cells. As cells use up oxygen, the concentration of oxygen inside becomes lower than the concentration outside. So oxygen diffuses in through the cell membrane and into the cell. Similarly,

as waste carbon dioxide builds up inside the cell, its concentration becomes higher than outside. Carbon dioxide then diffuses out through the cell membrane.

Diffusion is the key to gas exchange. Large animals with lots of cells, such as people, have respiratory systems in which oxygen and carbon dioxide diffuse in and out of the blood. As it moves through the body, blood comes into contact with body cells. Blood transports gases between the cells and the respiratory organs, the lungs.

GAS EXCHANGE

Air enters the nose or mouth and goes down a tube called the trachea. It splits into tubelike branches called the bronchi (singular bronchus). The bronchi then enter the lungs, where they branch into even smaller tubes called the bronchioles.

Gas exchange occurs in the lung cells. Lungs contain large numbers of clusters of air sacs called alveoli (singular alveolus). The alveoli bunch together like grapes at the tips of the bronchioles. Each bunch is called an alveolar sac. Because each sac contains many alveoli, the surface area available for gas exchange is enormous. The 600 million or so alveoli in a pair of human lungs have a surface area of around 750 square feet (68 square m)—enough to cover a tennis court.

People breathe in oxygen-rich air from the environment and breathe out air laden with carbon dioxide from inside their body. The two gases are constantly being exchanged inside the alveoli. The walls of an alveolus are only one cell thick to help swift diffusion. They are also elastic to allow easy movement of gases in and out of the air sac. Alveoli contain a network of vessels called capillaries that carry blood through the lungs.

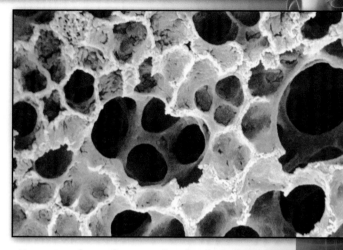

A section through some alveoli. Their thin walls are just one cell in thickness. Up to 600 million alveoli occur in a person's lungs.

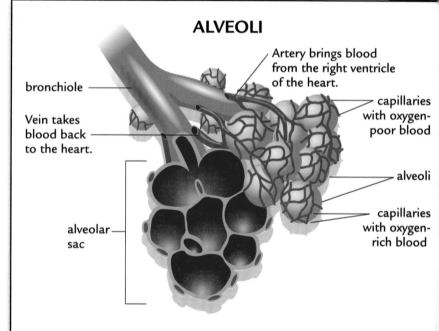

ALVEOLI

bronchiole

Vein takes blood back to the heart.

alveolar sac

Artery brings blood from the right ventricle of the heart.

capillaries with oxygen-poor blood

alveoli

capillaries with oxygen-rich blood

Gas exchange occurs between the blood in the capillaries and air in the alveoli. Gases move through the moist inner surface of the alveoli.

SINISTER SMOG

Smog contains substances called pollutants that damage people's health and the environment. They include a gas called ozone, which can make breathing difficult and painful. Smog can be deadly to people suffering from respiratory diseases such as asthma.

Most smog and ozone come from car exhausts. Sport utility vehicles (SUVs) produce the most smog and ozone. But automobile manufacturers have yet to make SUVs more environmentally friendly. Do you think these companies should be forced to build SUVs that produce less pollution? Or should SUV owners pay a "pollution" tax to encourage people to drive less damaging cars?

Smog over Los Angeles is caused by pollutants.

OXYGEN-POOR AND OXYGEN-RICH BLOOD

Blood that enters the lungs from the heart has already made its rounds through the body, collecting waste products. The concentration of carbon dioxide in this blood is high, while the carbon dioxide concentration in the alveoli is low. So carbon dioxide diffuses out of the blood and into the alveoli. From the alveoli the carbon dioxide leaves the body along the same route that air from outside enters. It is breathed out through the nose and mouth.

The blood that gives up its carbon dioxide is oxygen poor, but it picks up oxygen as it flows through the capillaries surrounding the alveoli. Once the

BREATHING IN FINE PARTICLES

When you breathe in, fine particles 100 times thinner than a human hair from coalburning power plants may enter your lungs along with oxygen and other gases. These fine particles make breathing problems worse and cause an estimated 150,000 early deaths from lung disease every year. Many people want regulations to limit powerplant emissions, but some think that such regulations will make electricity too expensive.

SAVING ENERGY

Moving around costs energy. Animals use a range of strategies to limit energy wasted by breathing while swimming, running, or flying. For example, when penguins and dolphins swim long distances, they occasionally leap from the water. This behavior is called porpoising. Porpoising does not help these animals travel faster, but it does allow them to breathe while maintaining their speed. Another neat trick is used by animals such as kangaroos, horses, and dogs. Biologists have found that these beasts take one breath per step as they run or hop. At speed they use the motion of organs inside them such as the liver to breathe. The movement shifts the diaphragm. That allows the animal to breathe without wasting energy on muscular movements of the ribs and diaphragm, as people must do.

Kangaroos (right) "vibrate" to breathe when they hop quickly. The motion of their internal organs moves the diaphragm, helping them save energy.

oxygen has diffused into the capillaries, it binds to a molecule called hemoglobin contained inside red blood cells. The oxygen-rich blood then flows from the lungs back to the heart, which pumps it through the rest of the body.

When oxygen-rich blood reaches the body cells, it has a greater concentration of oxygen than they do. So the gas diffuses out of the blood by passing through the capillary membranes and into the cells. At the same time, carbon dioxide from the cells diffuses into the blood. When the blood reenters the lungs, carbon dioxide diffuses through the alveoli and is breathed out of the body.

Cells use oxygen to respire. This involves a chemical reaction between a fuel, such as glucose, and the oxygen to produce energy.

HEMOGLOBIN

Hemoglobin is the substance in red blood cells that binds to and carries oxygen to body cells. Hemoglobin has a chemical "affinity" for oxygen—that is, hemoglobin absorbs many times more oxygen than do other molecules, such as water. In fact, hemoglobin allows blood to carry 70 times more oxygen than it otherwise could. Hemoglobin is essential for efficient oxygen transport.

CIGARETTES AND BREATHING

Smoking cigarettes and other tobacco products damages the lungs and causes fatal diseases. Antismoking regulations are becoming more common and widespread. In many places smoking is now banned in public places, such as bars, restaurants, and sports stadiums. Second-hand cigarette smoke breathed out by smokers may harm people nearby. This is called passive smoking. Yet most smokers claim they have a right to smoke cigarettes, especially in outside places where the smoke can disperse in the air. Do you think that there is a point at which antismoking laws interfere with a citizen's right to smoke if he or she wants to? Or do you think that something that could damage other people's health should be banned outright?

THE LUNGS

Human lungs are large, triangular organs that are broader at the bottom than at the top. They are enclosed in two baglike membranes called pleurae (sing. pleura). The inner pleura attaches to the spongy tissue of the lungs. The outer pleura is a stronger, tougher protective membrane. The lungs are protected further by the rib cage, which surrounds them.

BREATHE IN, BREATHE OUT

At the base of the lungs lies the diaphragm, a strong, elastic muscle that controls breathing. The diaphragm forms a partition between the chest and the abdomen. When relaxed, the diaphragm is domed and curves upward to rest in the chest. When the diaphragm contracts, it flattens and moves lower, increasing the volume of the rib cage, which sucks air

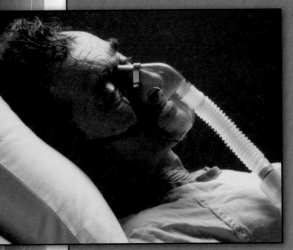

VENTILATORS

A mechanical ventilator is a machine that "breathes" for someone with breathing problems. A ventilator monitors the flow of gases in and out of the patient. Oxygen flows from a container, through tubes, and into the patient's lungs. The machine controls the exact amount and pressure. It regulates the airflow carefully, so the lungs are not expanded too much or too little, and the alveoli are not damaged. The rate of breathing is also controlled, so breathing in and out occurs at normal intervals.

DIFFICULT BREATHING

Some lung diseases—such as an illness called emphysema caused by smoking—destroy lung tissue or make the alveoli unable to absorb oxygen. To get an idea of the effects of destroyed lung tissue, get a drinking straw, and put one end between your lips (right). Close your lips tightly around the straw. For one full minute breathe in and out only through the straw. This will give you some idea how it feels to have a lung disease such as emphysema.

into the lungs. The contraction of the muscles between the ribs causes the rib cage to lift and move out, increasing the volume of the lungs and also causing air to enter them from the bronchi.

When the diaphragm and rib cage muscles relax, the ribs move back, down, and in. The volume of the lungs decreases, and air is forced out of the body. The person then breathes out. The diaphragm resumes its domed position inside the chest, ready for the next breath.

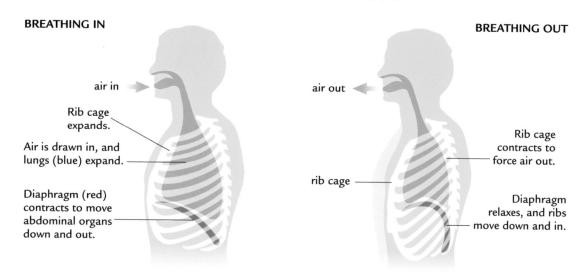

BREATHING IN AND OUT

BREATHING IN

air in

Rib cage expands.

Air is drawn in, and lungs (blue) expand.

Diaphragm (red) contracts to move abdominal organs down and out.

BREATHING OUT

air out

Rib cage contracts to force air out.

rib cage

Diaphragm relaxes, and ribs move down and in.

CHAPTER FIVE

THE SKELETOMUSCULAR SYSTEM

The bones form a framework for the body called the skeleton. Muscles are bundles of fibers that are attached to the bones. The muscles and bones work together to allow you to move.

The main functions of the skeleton are to provide support to the body, to anchor attached muscles and thus allow movement, to protect vital internal organs, and to create a constant supply of blood cells.

THE SKELETON

Your skeleton has two main parts. One is called the axial skeleton, which includes the cranium (skull), the vertebral column (backbone), and the rib cage. The other is called the appendicular skeleton, which includes the bones of the limbs, the hips, and the shoulders.

An animal's appendicular skeleton determines how it moves—for example, whether it walks on two or four legs, runs, swims, or flies.

Bones meet at joints, of which there are several kinds. Different joints allow the bones to move in different directions. Some joints, such as most in your skull, permit no movement at all. You might have muscles that allow you to wiggle your ears, but there is no way you can flex your skull.

Arm wrestlers try to outcompete each other. They are using their arm muscles and bones to prove who is the strongest.

THE STRUCTURE OF BONE

The human skeleton is made of a hard tissue called bone. Although bones vary in size and shape, they all have a similar structure. Bone consists mainly of inorganic materials, such as calcium and phosphorus, and protein fibers called collagen. Inorganic materials are those that do not contain carbon. Calcium and phosphorus give bone its strength and hardness. Collagen fibers give bone its flexibility. Bone cells, called osteocytes, are embedded in a mass of minerals and collagen fibers. Osteocytes are living cells,

and they are surrounded by a network of tiny blood vessels called capillaries.

Most bone has three layers. The outer, protective layer is called the periosteum. It is the layer from which new bone forms. The periosteum is riddled with blood vessels and nerve endings. When you break a bone, the pain you feel comes from nerves in the periosteum.

Beneath the periosteum lies the white, rock-hard compact bone that supports the body's weight. Compact bone

Major bones of the human body. Our 206 bones include 22 in the skull and, although skull bones are fused together in adults, they are still counted as 22 separate bones.

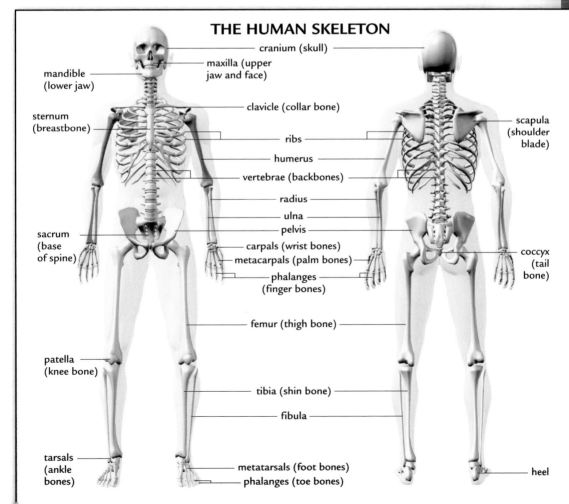

THE HUMAN SKELETON

cranium (skull)

maxilla (upper jaw and face)

mandible (lower jaw)

clavicle (collar bone)

sternum (breastbone)

scapula (shoulder blade)

ribs

humerus

vertebrae (backbones)

radius

ulna

pelvis

sacrum (base of spine)

carpals (wrist bones)

metacarpals (palm bones)

coccyx (tail bone)

phalanges (finger bones)

femur (thigh bone)

patella (knee bone)

tibia (shin bone)

fibula

tarsals (ankle bones)

metatarsals (foot bones)

heel

phalanges (toe bones)

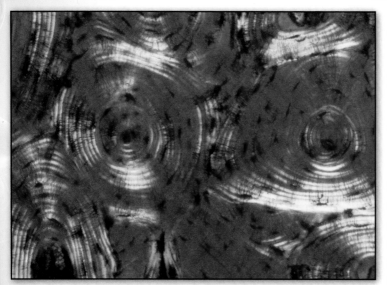

A cross section through compact bone. Bone has a distinctive appearance—like layers of circles or tree rings. The small dark ovals are osteocytes (a type of bone cell).

contains a network of tiny chambers, each of which contains an osteocyte.

The innermost and least dense layer of bone is called spongy bone, or bone marrow. This layer is where blood cells are produced. Spongy bone contains two types of marrow. Red marrow produces blood cells, while yellow marrow stores fat.

HOW BONES GROW

Bone is constantly being broken down and rebuilt. Three types of bone cells are involved in this process. Osteoclasts break down and dissolve old and damaged bones. Osteoblasts make new bone tissue. Osteocytes maintain the right amount of calcium and phosphorus in newly created bone.

Leg and arm bones grow, or elongate (get longer), from sites called growth plates. They are near the ends of the bones. A white, flexible tissue called cartilage occurs at the growth plates. Connective tissue forms around the cartilage, eventually turning it into compact bone. Blood vessels extend from the bone marrow into the developing bone. Bone formation continues throughout childhood. When you reach

EXOSKELETONS

Many invertebrates (animals without backbones) such as insects and crabs have an exoskeleton. It is a hard casing on the outside of the body. The exoskeleton serves three major functions—it protects the body, serves as an attachment point for muscles, and helps reduce water loss. Exoskeletons cannot usually expand, though. In order to grow, the animal makes a new exoskeleton under the old one. The old skin is then shed in a process called molting. The animal quickly expands while the new exoskeleton is soft. This can be a dangerous time for the temporarily unprotected animal. It must wait for the new exoskeleton to harden before it regains its protective covering.

your full height and your bones are fully shaped, bone elongation stops. Although adult bones do not elongate, they can be strengthened by exercise.

THE SKULL, BACKBONE, AND RIBS

Your skull contains 29 bones, but most of them (especially those at the top) are fused together. The skull is made of thick, hard bone and protects the body's control center—the brain. The only bones in the skull that move are the jaw and the tiny bones of the middle ear. The jaw is hinged to the skull and can move up and down and, to a lesser extent, sideways. This movable jaw enables people to eat and to communicate with each other.

The backbone, or vertebral column, protects the spinal cord, which is made up of nerves carrying vital messages to and from the brain. The backbone is made up of a series of 33 bones called vertebrae (singular vertebra). The

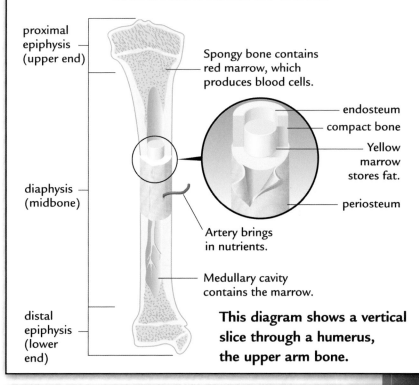

THE STRUCTURE OF BONE

proximal epiphysis (upper end)

diaphysis (midbone)

distal epiphysis (lower end)

Spongy bone contains red marrow, which produces blood cells.

endosteum

compact bone

Yellow marrow stores fat.

periosteum

Artery brings in nutrients.

Medullary cavity contains the marrow.

This diagram shows a vertical slice through a humerus, the upper arm bone.

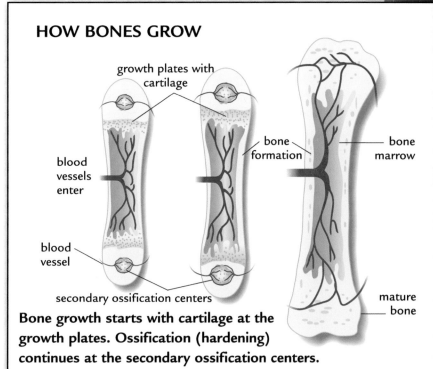

HOW BONES GROW

growth plates with cartilage

blood vessels enter

blood vessel

secondary ossification centers

bone formation

bone marrow

mature bone

Bone growth starts with cartilage at the growth plates. Ossification (hardening) continues at the secondary ossification centers.

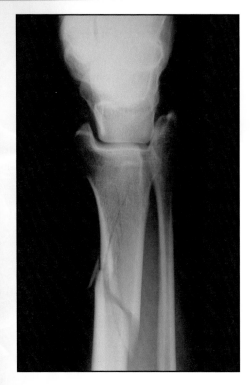

An X-ray showing a simple tibia of the leg. Casts of plaster are used to hold the two broken bone ends in place so they can knit together correctly.

backbone meet at a joint that allows the head to move up and down and side to side.

The rib cage consists of the sternum and 12 pairs of ribs. Each pair of ribs is attached to one of the vertebrae in the backbone. The sternum consists of three bones that together are also called the breastbone.

THE PELVIC AND PECTORAL GIRDLES AND LEG AND ARM BONES

The appendicular skeleton consists of the pelvic girdle (hip bones) and leg bones, the pectoral girdle (shoulder blades and collar bones), and arm bones. The bones in the pelvic girdle allow limited movement. There are six pairs of mostly fused bones, plus some of the lower vertebrae, in the adult pelvic girdle. The pelvic bones are fused to help strengthen the pelvic girdle. This provides more protection for the pelvic organs.

The femur (thighbone) meets the pelvic girdle at the hip socket. This joint is formed by three fused pelvic bones. Going down the leg, the femur is

backbone permits a degree of movement, allowing you to bend and twist. The spinal cord enters the brain at an opening in the base of the skull. The skull and the

OSTEOPOROSIS

One out of two women and one out of eight men experience bone loss as they get older. This condition is called osteoporosis. It can arise as a result of lack of exercise, a calcium-poor diet, or the hormonal changes that occur during and after menopause (when menstruation stops). Some doctors state that osteoporosis can be prevented if children and young adults keep up a lifelong routine of regular exercise and eat a diet rich in calcium or take calcium supplements to prevent bone loss later in life. How would you alter your diet and daily life to help prevent osteoporosis when you grow older?

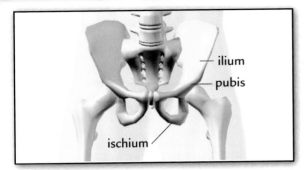

The pelvic girdle. The hip bones actually consist of three bones. They are fused to provide strength and support for the organs inside.

connected to the knee bone, then to the shin bones (tibia and fibula) and then to the bones of the ankle and foot.

Your body's other girdle—the pectoral girdle—consists of your two shoulder blades (called scapulae) and two collar bones (called clavicles). The scapulae (singular scapula) are flat, thick bones ideal for the attachment of strong arm muscles. The clavicles meet the scapulae on the front side of the shoulder joint. The clavicles join in the middle of the sternum. Also joined to the scapulae are the upper arm bone (humerus), the bones of the forearm (radius and ulna), and the bones of the wrist and hand.

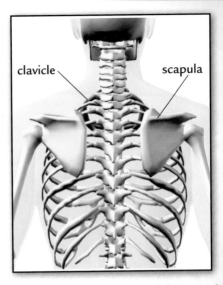

The pectoral girdle consists of the scapulae and clavicles.

TYPES OF JOINTS

Most bones meet at joints—connections that allow the bones to move a certain amount in one or more directions. There are three types of joints: immovable, partly movable, and synovial joints.

Immovable joints consist of fused bones, as in the skull. Partly movable joints like those between the vertebrae often have cartilage between them and

ARTIFICIAL BONES AND JOINTS

When they are injured or diseased, entire bones or joints sometimes need to be replaced. Surgeons remove the old joint or bone (often a hip or knee) and implant a new one. In the 1920s implants were made of stainless steel. By the 1950s manufacturers of implants used pure titanium, another metal. Both materials were problematic. Body fluids damaged them, and they were not very strong or long lasting. The latest implants are made of a combination of the metals nickel and titanium called nitinol. Nitinol is not eroded by the body, and it is strong and flexible.

HOW JOINTS FUNCTION

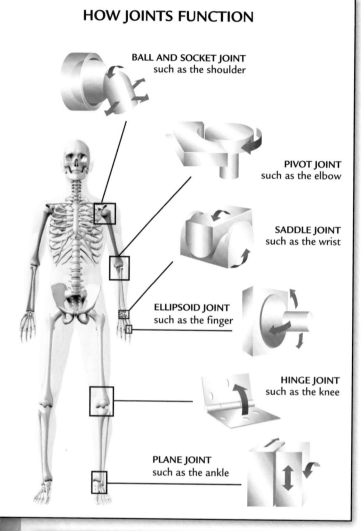

BALL AND SOCKET JOINT
such as the shoulder

PIVOT JOINT
such as the elbow

SADDLE JOINT
such as the wrist

ELLIPSOID JOINT
such as the finger

HINGE JOINT
such as the knee

PLANE JOINT
such as the ankle

Different joints in the body allow different degrees of freedom, as shown by the arrows in this diagram.

are flexible in limited directions. Synovial joints, such as those of the shoulders, allow for a wider range of movement. Joints prevent the grinding of bone against bone when you move. Where two bones meet at a joint, there are extremely smooth layers of cartilage. Synovial joints also produce a lubricant (slippery substance) called synovial fluid. The fluid serves to lubricate all parts of the joint. Bones that meet at a joint are held together by tough ligaments. Ligaments are a type of tough connective tissue. When people damage a ligament, they are said to have a "sprain."

TYPES OF MUSCLES

Muscles are bundles of fibers most of which are attached to and pull on your bones.

BIOFEEDBACK

Biofeedback is a technique in which you learn how to control body processes that you cannot normally consciously affect. You are connected to an electronic monitoring machine via electrodes (electric sensors) taped to your body. A monitor shows your blood pressure, heartbeat, temperature, and brain activity. A biofeedback expert teaches you how to relax your muscles and control your breathing as you watch the effects on the monitor. In time you learn to use these relaxation techniques without the monitor. This lowers your blood pressure.

SMART PROSTHESES

A prosthesis is an artificial body part, such as an arm or a leg. Wooden legs replace limbs but do not work as well as the original. Some modern prostheses, however, behave more like living limbs and respond to electrical impulses the way muscles do. The prostheses are controlled by sophisticated electronics in contact with the user's own muscle and with sensors in the prosthesis. The sensors detect tiny electrical signals in the human muscle and transmit the signal to the artificial limb. This artificial limb is powered by batteries and moves the prosthesis in a way similar to natural limb movement.

In this way they move your body. They can do so because muscle cells are master shape shifters. They change their shape by squeezing (contracting); they never push.

There are three basic types of muscles—smooth muscle, skeletal muscle, and cardiac muscle. Smooth muscles line most of your internal organs, such as your stomach, intestines, and blood vessels. These muscles move without you willing them to because they are controlled by the autonomic nervous system.

Skeletal muscles attach to the bones that they move. They are also called voluntary muscles (because they are under your control most of the time) or striated muscles (because under a microscope they look striated, or striped). Cardiac (heart) muscles are involuntary muscles, but the heart has its own system of internal controls. The muscles of the heart are unique in that they

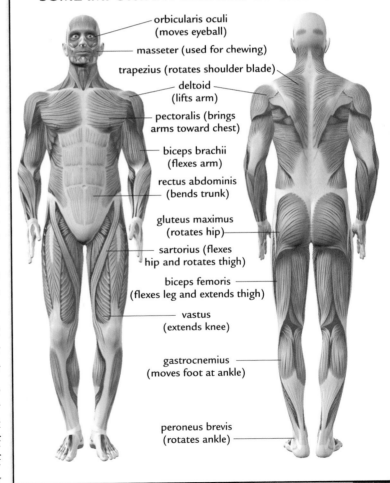

SOME IMPORTANT MUSCLES OF THE BODY

orbicularis oculi
(moves eyeball)

masseter (used for chewing)

trapezius (rotates shoulder blade)

deltoid
(lifts arm)

pectoralis (brings arms toward chest)

biceps brachii
(flexes arm)

rectus abdominis
(bends trunk)

gluteus maximus
(rotates hip)

sartorius (flexes hip and rotates thigh)

biceps femoris
(flexes leg and extends thigh)

vastus
(extends knee)

gastrocnemius
(moves foot at ankle)

peroneus brevis
(rotates ankle)

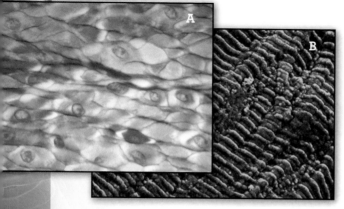

A.) Smooth muscle tissue from the inner wall of a human stomach.

B.) This is a section of heart, or cardiac, muscle under the microscope.

bind together to form a dense collagen tissue called a tendon. Tendons attach at one end to voluntary muscle and at the other to the bone that the muscle moves.

MUSCLES WORKING IN TANDEM

Most skeletal muscles work by opposing the actions of other muscles. Thus, when one muscle contracts, its opposite (the antagonist muscle) relaxes and is stretched (see below). For example, when you lift something with your arm, nerve signals from the brain travel to your arm muscles and tell the muscles on the front of your upper arm—the biceps—to contract, or flex. At the same time, the

have characteristics of both smooth muscles and skeletal muscles.

Most muscles are attached directly to the bones in your skeleton. Many of your lip and face muscles, however, are not attached directly to bone. All skeletal muscles have lots of sensory nerves that tell the brain what a muscle is doing.

Skeletal muscle cells are also called muscle fibers. Muscle fibers are strongly bound in a bundle called a fasicle. Fasicles are tied together and covered by a strong casing of connective tissue called the fascia. At the ends of a muscle the fascia

MUSCLE ANTAGONISM

Muscles often work in tandem to get a job done. This is called muscle antagonism. The muscles work around a pivot point, or fulcrum. The pull of one muscle (effort) is opposed by resistance from another (load).

The lower part of the diagram shows where the forces are operating.

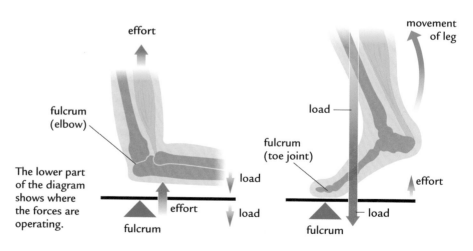

opposing muscle to the biceps on the back of your arm—the triceps—relaxes and extends to allow your arm to bend. In this example the muscle that contracts is called the flexor muscle, and the muscle that relaxes is called the extensor muscle. If, while you are contracting one muscle, you do not let its antagonist muscle relax, the muscles simply bulge.

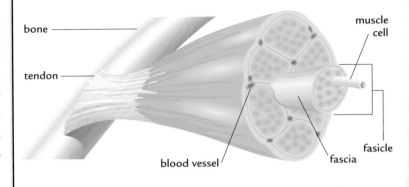

STRUCTURE OF SKELETAL MUSCLE

bone

tendon

blood vessel

fascia

fasicle

muscle cell

MUSCLES RESPOND TO SIGNALS

Muscles contract when they receive electrical signals from the brain and other parts of the central nervous system. The signals travel from the brain along nerves called motor neurons, a type of nerve cell, that lead from the spinal cord to muscles. The neurons release a chemical that makes the muscle contract.

skull

fulcrum (base of skull)

muscles

effort

load

movement of face

fulcrum

STEROIDS

Some athletes and bodybuilders take artificial chemicals, called anabolic steroids, to improve the size and strength of their muscles. Anabolic steroids are related to naturally occurring chemicals called hormones that are present in the body. Using anabolic steroids that have not been prescribed by a doctor is illegal and very dangerous. Yet the pressure to excel at sports or to look big and strong tempts some people to abuse anabolic steroids. Despite their side effects (acne, liver damage, and aggression), some athletes feel they must take steroids to compete.

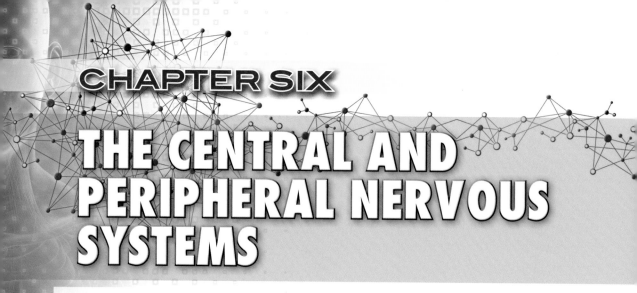

CHAPTER SIX

THE CENTRAL AND PERIPHERAL NERVOUS SYSTEMS

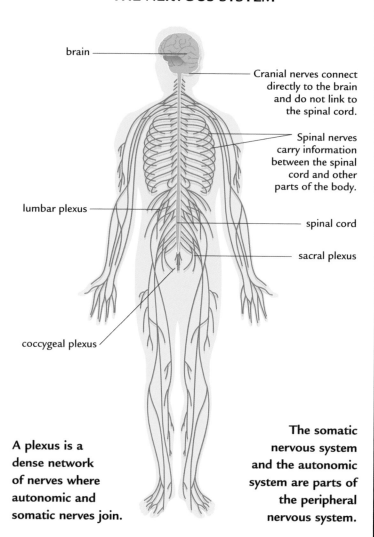

THE NERVOUS SYSTEM

brain

Cranial nerves connect directly to the brain and do not link to the spinal cord.

Spinal nerves carry information between the spinal cord and other parts of the body.

lumbar plexus

spinal cord

sacral plexus

coccygeal plexus

A plexus is a dense network of nerves where autonomic and somatic nerves join.

The somatic nervous system and the autonomic system are parts of the peripheral nervous system.

Your nervous system is a huge network of 100 billion nerve cells. It coordinates how you react to events that take place around you.

The nervous system senses the outside world and helps you react to events there by thinking, moving, and speaking. It also regulates many functions inside your body, such as breathing and heart rate. Nerves contain bundles of thousands of nerve cells, or neurons. They transmit messages in the form of electrical signals that travel along their length.

Your nervous system has two main parts. They are called the

The central nervous system (CNS) is shown in red; the peripheral nervous system (PNS) is shown in blue.

THE STRUCTURE OF A MOTOR NEURON

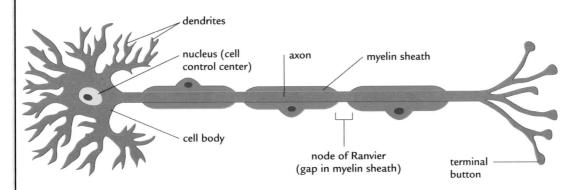

- dendrites
- nucleus (cell control center)
- axon
- myelin sheath
- cell body
- node of Ranvier (gap in myelin sheath)
- terminal button

Motor neurons carry electrical signals from the central nervous system to muscles and glands.

Motor neurons are nerve cells that carry signals from the brain to organs, tissues, and glands. Each has a cell body, a long extension called an axon, and shorter extensions called dendrites.

central nervous system and the peripheral nervous system. The central nervous system, or CNS, is made up of the brain and a collection of nerve cells called the spinal cord that run along the back to the brain. The CNS also contains cells called glia that nourish and protect the neurons.

The CNS acts as the body's control and processing unit. The peripheral nervous system, or PNS, is different.

It consists of a network of nerves that spread from the central nervous system to other parts of the body. The PNS has two main parts, the somatic nervous system and the autonomic nervous system. The somatic system is concerned with the outside world and your reactions to it. It

A nerve contains many axons, each wrapped by a myelin sheath. The axons are grouped into fasicles.

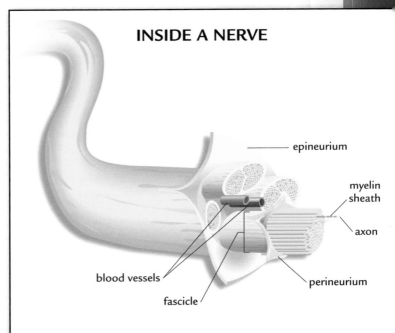

INSIDE A NERVE

- epineurium
- myelin sheath
- axon
- blood vessels
- perineurium
- fascicle

RUBBING TO REDUCE PAIN

Have you ever wondered why, when you stub your toe or bang your elbow, rubbing the injured area extremely vigorously can limit the pain a little? Rubbing like this stimulates vast numbers of sensory receptors. They send a barrage of signals to the brain. The jumble of signals makes it difficult for your brain to perceive the pain.

STRUCTURE OF THE SPINAL CORD

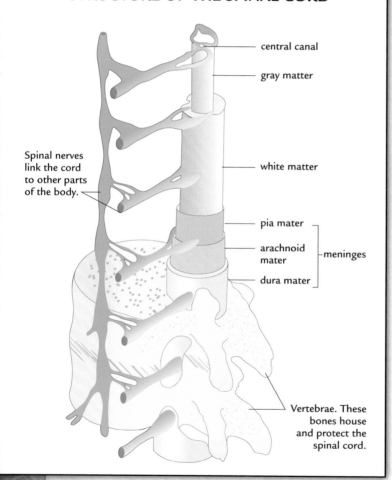

central canal

gray matter

Spinal nerves link the cord to other parts of the body.

white matter

pia mater

arachnoid mater

meninges

dura mater

Vertebrae. These bones house and protect the spinal cord.

A section through the spinal cord. White and gray matter make up the cord. These are surrounded by membranes called meninges.

gathers information from your sense organs and sends this information to the CNS. It also carries signals from the CNS to the muscles attached to parts of your skeleton, allowing you to make conscious movements.

The autonomic system regulates the internal workings of your body. It carries information from the body to the CNS and transmits signals from the brain to organs such as the heart. Nerve cells that carry information toward the CNS are called sensory neurons. Those that carry signals from the CNS to organs such as muscles are called motor neurons.

AUTOMATIC REFLEX ACTION

To a large extent your nervous system works automatically by reflex action. A reflex is a predictable, automatic response of the nervous system to an event (called a stimulus) outside or inside the body. Many reflexes operate by means of nerve connections in the spinal

TESTING RESPONSE TIMES

Hold a ruler at one end, and let it hang down vertically. Have a friend put his or her hand near the bottom of the ruler with the thumb and forefinger ready to grasp it but not touching it. Tell your friend that you will drop the ruler sometime within the next 5 seconds and that he or she must try to catch it as fast as possible. Record the place at which he or she catches the ruler. This measurement will give you an idea of your friend's response time. Try this three or four times, and figure out an average response time for your friend. Then reverse roles, and test your own response time. Is the result much different between you and your friend? Try the same test at different times of day—in the morning and in the evening—to see if there is any difference in the results.

cord and do not require any conscious involvement of the brain.

Most reflexes are defense mechanisms that protect you against injury, such as withdrawing your hand when it touches a hot surface. Some reflexes, such as blinking your eye, work by means of nerve cell connections in parts of your brain.

THE BRAIN'S STRUCTURE

Your brain is a soft, rounded mass about the size of a large grapefruit. It contains two main types of tissue, called gray matter and white matter. Gray matter is mainly made up of the cell bodies of billions of interconnected nerve cells. White matter consists mainly of nerve cell fibers—cabling that connects different parts of the brain. Protective glial cells are distributed throughout the brain.

This physician is testing the reflexes of a patient. A sharp tap just below the kneecap leads to a "knee-jerk" reflex.

At the base of the brain is a structure called the brainstem. This stalklike organ connects the brain to the spinal cord. The brainstem is made up of three parts called the medulla, the pons, and the midbrain. The brainstem helps regulate automatic body functions such as the heartbeat and breathing. Behind the brainstem is a structure called the cerebellum. This

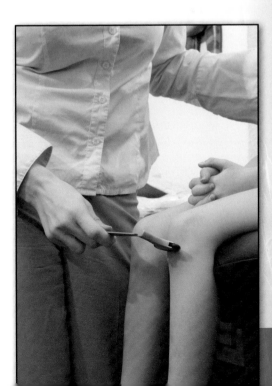

HOW DO NERVES WORK?

RESTING STAGE

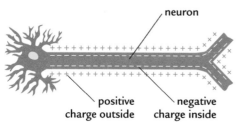

neuron

positive charge outside

negative charge inside

In its resting state the inside of a neuron is negatively charged. That is due to the presence of negative particles, or ions.

DEPOLARIZATION

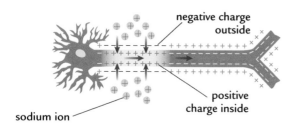

negative charge outside

positive charge inside

sodium ion

During a nerve impulse positive ions of sodium flood in. They switch the charge inside the cell to positive. This depolarization sweeps along the neuron.

REPOLARIZATION

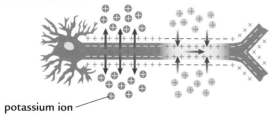

potassium ion

Once the impulse passes, positive potassium ions move out of the cell. This repolarization makes the inside of the cell negative again.

structure helps control posture and balance, and it also coordinates movements. Thanks to your cerebellum, you can stand upright, keep your balance, and move around.

The uppermost and largest part of the brain is called the cerebrum. It is split into two halves called the cerebral hemispheres. They are joined by a thick band of nerve cell fibers called the corpus callosum. The surface of each hemisphere is heavily folded, so the cerebrum looks a little like a huge walnut. The folds increase the area available for neurons. This outer part of the brain consists of gray matter and is called the cerebral cortex. The cortex is where advanced brain activities, such as thought and recognition of speech, take place.

Above the brainstem and between the two cerebral hemispheres are several other brain parts. They include the thalamus, which contains some

FEEL YOUR FUNNY BONE

Your "funny bone" is actually a nerve called the ulnar nerve. To feel it, bend your left arm, and feel the tip of your elbow with your right hand. Running through the space between the elbow tip and a smaller bony lump below it, you will feel a firm cord—the ulnar nerve. Push the cord gently. You will feel a similar (though less painful) sensation as when you bump your "funny bone" against a hard object by accident.

BRAIN CELL TRANSPLANTS

Surgeons have the capability of transferring human brain cells, a few million at a time, from one person's brain to another. That can help reduce the symptoms of certain brain illnesses. Scientists have also transplanted cells from the brains of pigs into humans.

There are many concerns regarding these transplants. Transported human brain cells are often tumor cells (cells growing out of control). However, scientists have developed a way of changing these rapidly dividing cells into nondividing ones before transplantation begins.

With pig cell transplants concerns have been raised that animals such as pigs may be turned into "spare parts" factories. There are also worries about new diseases being transferred from animals to humans.

THE STRUCTURE OF THE BRAIN

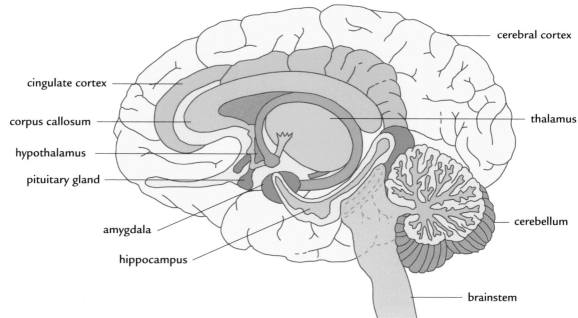

This vertical slice through the brain shows the main structures inside.

BRAIN DEATH

The brainstem controls parts of the body such as the heart. With advances in medical technology physicians can sometimes keep these body parts working even when the brainstem has ceased to function. A new way of recognizing death, called brain death, was developed in the 1970s. Brain death occurs when the whole brain, including the brainstem, stops functioning, and there is no hope of getting it working again. Most doctors accept that a brain-dead person has died—there is no point in keeping that person's heart pumping. Others are uncomfortable with brain death since it goes against traditional ideas about death.

areas involved in memory and movement; the pituitary gland, which produces many hormones and is an important part of the endocrine system; the hypothalamus, which forms a link between the nervous system and the endocrine system; and the limbic system, a collection of brain structures involved in functions such as memory, emotion, instinctive behavior, and sense of smell.

The brain uses up oxygen and nutrients at a fast rate in order to function, and for this reason it needs a large supply of blood. Numerous small blood vessels run throughout the brain. They are supplied

DOES HEADING THE BALL CAUSE DAMAGE?

There have been some news reports of professional soccer players who have suffered brain damage that has led to death as a result of "heading" the ball. Although this is a cause for concern, many of the affected people played soccer decades ago, when heavy leather balls were used. When wet, these balls grew heavier and heavier. The lighter soccer balls used today are much less risky. Experts say that to minimize any risk, soccer players should get instruction on how to head the ball correctly—with the forehead, not the top of the head—and children should use a size of ball appropriate to their age.

by four large arteries that run up through the neck. If the blood supply to your brain were to be cut off for any reason, you would lose consciousness within ten seconds. After just a few minutes your brain would be permanently damaged.

LOBES OF THE CORTEX

Each of the brain's hemispheres contains four main regions called lobes. They are the frontal lobe (at the front), the occipital lobe (at the back), the temporal lobe (at the side), and the parietal lobe (on the upper side behind the frontal lobe). The cortex that covers each lobe has specific functions. For example, parts of the temporal lobe play a role in hearing; a large area of the frontal lobe (called the motor cortex) controls body movements; and a strip of the parietal lobe is involved in the sense of touch.

Different parts of the cortex often work together. For example, when you see someone you know, one part of the brain recognizes that person's face, and another finds the person's name in your memory. A third area analyzes your feelings about

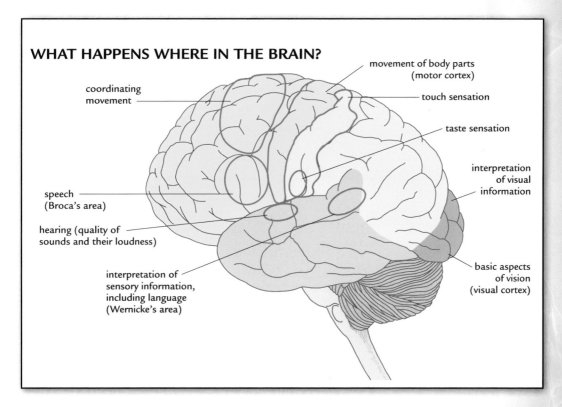

WHAT HAPPENS WHERE IN THE BRAIN?

- movement of body parts (motor cortex)
- coordinating movement
- touch sensation
- taste sensation
- interpretation of visual information
- speech (Broca's area)
- hearing (quality of sounds and their loudness)
- interpretation of sensory information, including language (Wernicke's area)
- basic aspects of vision (visual cortex)

Different functions of the brain take place at different locations on the cortex. This diagram also shows the four main lobes of the brain. The frontal lobe is yellow; the parietal lobe is pink; the temporal lobe is light blue; and the occipital lobe is dark blue.

that person and whether you would like to call out a greeting. A fourth figures out the form of the greeting, and a fifth produces the exact sequence of nerve signals to muscles in your chest, neck, mouth, and lips to say "hello."

Some brain functions are shared equally between the two sides of the cerebrum. For example, there is a motor cortex on each side. Each motor cortex controls movements on the opposite side of the body. Other functions, such as language, are handled on one side of the brain called the dominant hemisphere.

In nearly all right-handed people, and in about two-thirds of left-handed people, the left cerebral hemisphere is the dominant hemisphere. In most people the left hemisphere is also the one used for mathematical skills.

The nondominant hemisphere is important in spatial skills. People who suffer mild damage to the nondominant hemisphere may find they have problems when trying to read maps, or they may have trouble putting clothes on the right way around.

A complex activity, such as playing the piano, requires an enormous amount of nervous activity in the brain and in the rest of the nervous system.

RIGHT OR LEFT

Most people are either right handed (86 percent) or left handed (9 percent), but 5 percent of people are ambidextrous—equally gifted with either hand. To test whether a young child is right or left handed, they are given a task, such as dealing a deck of cards or throwing a ball, to see which hand they use. As well as handedness, people also tend to be better with one foot, eye, and even ear than the other.

TRICKING THE BRAIN

Cross your index and middle fingers on one hand to form a V shape. Now lightly rub the crossed tips of the two fingers up and down your nose. It will feel as if you have two noses! Your brain is confused by the information coming from the sides of the fingertips, which are in opposite positions from normal. To make sense of the information, the shape recognition area in your brain decides that two noses must be present!

STORING AND RECALLING INFORMATION

One of the most important of your brain's functions is the ability to memorize information and later recall (bring back) this information from memory. Your brain retains a memory not just of facts, such as your name and home address, but also the meanings of those words and what those words sound and look like, the shapes and colors of objects, and so on. The brain also keeps a memory of events in your past and whether those events were pleasant or unpleasant, and it memorizes skills, such as how to walk or play the piano. The process of memorizing information and skills, and modifying those memories through experience, is called learning.

Scientists do not understand exactly how memories are stored in the brain, but they do know that there are two different types of memory storage systems. Short-term memory is for information you have just been told, such as a phone number. It is limited and lasts only for a short time. Information about important events and skills or facts

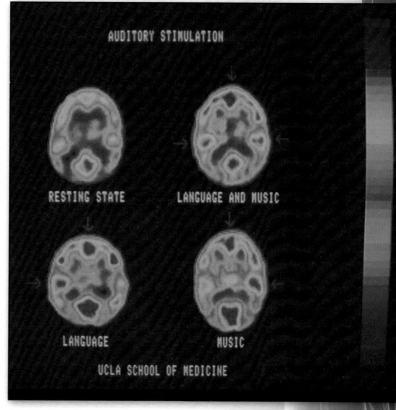

These are scans showing brain activity. They show that different stimuli, such as music or spoken language, trigger activity in different parts of the brain.

MEMORY AIDS

Your brain is better at storing information in visual form rather than, say, as strings of numbers. To remember something, it can help to fix an image in your mind related to the thing to be remembered. For example, to remember which months have 31 days, put your knuckles together. Then, starting on your first knuckle, count off the knuckles and spaces in between, saying the months in order. All the months with 31 days are on knuckles! Another trick can be to make up a phrase using the initial letters of words in the phrase to remember something. To remember the order of the classification groupings used in biology (kingdom, phylum, class, order, family, genus, species), you might use a phrase that conjures up an image, such as "kings prefer chatting on fancy green sofas." This is called a mnemonic, or memory aid.

HOW THE PITUITARY GLAND WORKS

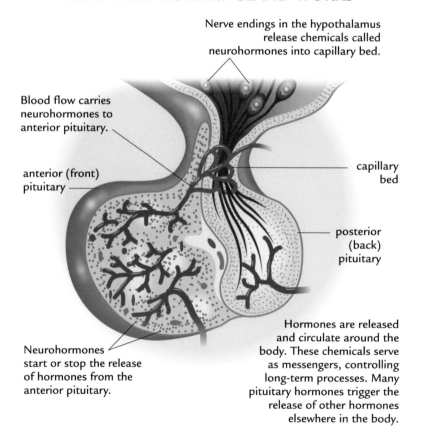

Nerve endings in the hypothalamus release chemicals called neurohormones into capillary bed.

Blood flow carries neurohormones to anterior pituitary.

anterior (front) pituitary

capillary bed

posterior (back) pituitary

Neurohormones start or stop the release of hormones from the anterior pituitary.

Hormones are released and circulate around the body. These chemicals serve as messengers, controlling long-term processes. Many pituitary hormones trigger the release of other hormones elsewhere in the body.

that you have learned by repetition go into a long-term memory bank. They generally stay with you for life.

HORMONES AND THE ENDOCRINE SYSTEM

There is a close link between the nervous system and another information network, the endocrine system. The endocrine system consists of glands located in different parts of the body. They secrete chemicals called hormones into the bloodstream. Hormones act as "messenger" chemicals. As they spread

NERVOUS SYSTEMS AND ROBOTS

The study of nervous systems is playing an increasing part in the design of robots. Robots have become more complex, with ever more sophisticated sensory systems and interconnected moving parts. Designers are finding it ever more challenging to build electronic systems that can handle and integrate all the different inputs and outputs. So they are studying systems that already cope with such challenges—the nervous systems of living organisms. Scientists are particularly interested in unraveling mechanisms that enable animal movement to be so smooth and coordinated.

This is a spider-bot. Its walking is controlled by a system similar to the human nervous system. This robot has been designed to walk on the surface of other planets.

through the body, they have specific effects on target tissues. These tissues are a long way away from the gland that released the hormone. Like the nervous system, the endocrine system is a control system. However, the endocrine system mostly regulates longer-term processes than those controlled by the nervous system. Examples of processes under endocrine control include growth and reproduction, the storage and use of energy in the body, the rate of blood cell production, and the maintenance of the body's water balance.

Much of the functioning of the endocrine system is controlled by the hypothalamus and the pituitary gland in the brain. Blood vessels carry hormones from the hypothalamus to the front part of the pituitary gland, where they trigger the release of other hormones. They in turn may cause other glands in the body to release hormones of their own. The back part of the pituitary also releases a number of hormones.

CHAPTER SEVEN

THE SENSORY SYSTEM

A person who has lost the sense of sight is guided by a specially trained dog. Deaf people are also helped by dogs that have been taught to alert them to sounds such as the doorbell ringing.

One of your body's most important functions is to make you aware of things that are happening all around you. Detecting changes in the world is the job of the senses, which are controlled by the brain.

The human body has developed five different ways of detecting information about the world. We call them the five senses, and they are sight, hearing, smell, taste, and touch.

The first four of the senses are concentrated within single organs of the body. The fifth sense, touch, is unique since it is carried out by sensitive cells throughout the whole body, especially the skin.

Detecting, or sensing, the world involves more than just the body's sense organs and sensitive cells. The nervous system carries the information that the senses detect to the brain. The brain is the body's nerve center, and it is constantly interpreting a large amount of sensory information and figuring out how to respond. A very large part of detecting what is happening in the world occurs in the brain rather than in the sense organs themselves.

SIGHT

The eyes are by far the most complex and important sense organs. You have two eyes. The brain combines the two slightly different images each eye generates to make a single, three-dimensional (3-D) view of the world. This is called stereoscopic or binocular vision. Each eye is made up of an eyeball attached to six different muscles that rotate the eyeball in a socket within the skull.

The eyeball works in a similar way as a camera. Light goes through the cornea, a transparent outer

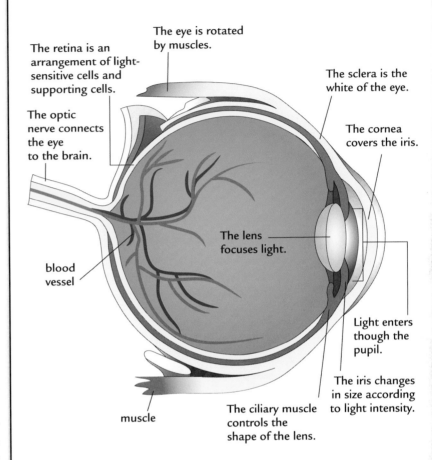

The retina is an arrangement of light-sensitive cells and supporting cells.

The eye is rotated by muscles.

The sclera is the white of the eye.

The optic nerve connects the eye to the brain.

The cornea covers the iris.

The lens focuses light.

blood vessel

Light enters though the pupil.

The iris changes in size according to light intensity.

muscle

The ciliary muscle controls the shape of the lens.

HOW MANY SENSES?

Most people believe they have only five senses, but it is possible there may be as many as 15 senses or more. While the classic five senses are concerned with detecting the outside world, the other senses tell the brain what is happening inside the body. Feelings such as hunger, tiredness, and balance are examples of these internal sense mechanisms. Small organs in the inner ear control balance. They detect movements of your head and feed signals back to your brain so it can order muscles in your body to move and help you keep your balance.

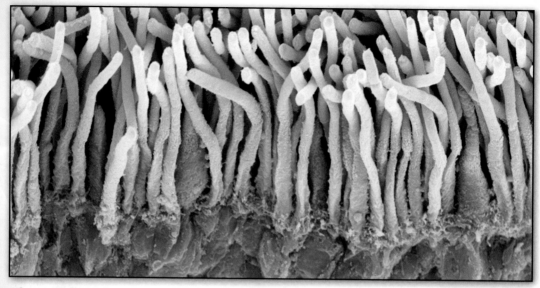

The retina lines the eyeball and is a very complicated system of nerve cells. It is made up of three layers. The first layer of light-sensitive cells, which contains rods and cones, is connected by two main branches of cells to another layer of cells that lead to the optic nerve.

lens of the eye, and the pupil, the black opening in the colored iris. The light is bent by a lens, travels through the vitreous humor (a clear gel that keeps the eyeball spherical), and arrives at the retina, a structure at the back of the eye.

The retina is like the photographic film in a camera. Sensory information from the retina is carried by the optic nerves (one from each eye) to the cerebral visual cortex, the part of the brain that decodes visual information. Together we call the eyes, the optic nerves, and the visual cortex the "visual system."

The retina is packed with two main types of cells. Some are shaped like rods and some like cones. These two cell types can detect different kinds of light. There are roughly 120 million rods and around

MACHINES THAT CAN SEE

One reason for studying human vision is to help design computers and robots that can "see." Many automatic processes, from sorting mail to examining tissue samples for cancer, are now carried out with the help of electronic vision. Electronic vision systems have two main parts in much the same way as human vision. One is a digital camera that detects light and translates it into an electronic code, much as our eyes detect light and send electrical nerve impulses to the brain. The other part is a computer system that analyzes the code and figures out what they are—it is like the visual cortex of our brain.

NIGHT SIGHT

Police officers and soldiers use night vision cameras to help them see in the dark. Just as your eyes are sensitive to the light things give off, these cameras detect an invisible kind of light called infrared radiation. Animals or people are warmer than their surroundings and show up as red or purple on infrared cameras. The face of the boy in the picture (right) is the warmest part of his body, while his hand appears to be the coldest.

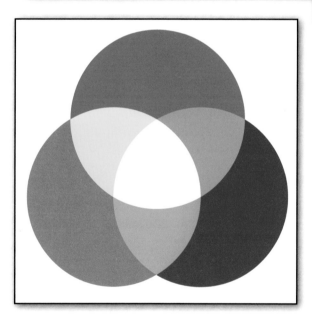

six million cones. The rods are sensitive mainly to gray shades and dim light, while the cones are sensitive to colored light. There are three types of cones, and each one is filled with a chemical that makes it most sensitive to either red, blue, or green light. The rods and cones are not distributed randomly over the retina. Most of the cones are packed into

With lights of the three primary colors of red, blue, and green you can get all the colors of a rainbow. Also, when lights of the three colors are mixed you see white light.

TEST YOUR RODS

Stare straight ahead. Without moving your head or eyes, concentrate on the things at the very edges of your field of view. You should not really be able to figure out the colors or shapes of these things, because that part of your vision is controlled by rod cells. Rods are poor at seeing details, and they do not detect colors.

REACHING OUT

Sit in front of a table that has different objects on it. Close one eye. Now without moving your head, try to reach out and touch different objects. Two eyes help us judge distances and locate things. See how much harder this is when you are using only one eye.

the center of the retina, called the fovea. The rods are arranged around the edge of the retina. That explains why your eyes see colors clearly in the center of what you look at (where there are most cones), and why you see dim objects or faint movements at the edges (where there are mostly rods).

If the visual system is damaged in some way, the result can be anything from disrupted sight to complete blindness. Cataracts are a common eye problem in which part of the lens stops letting the light through due to old age, injuries, or poor diet. People who are colorblind have trouble telling some colors apart because they lack one or more of the three types of cone cells.

Damage to parts of the brain that process visual information can lead to conditions called agnosias. People with an agnosia can see objects because their eyes work, but do not recognize the objects because the visual cortex in their brain is damaged.

HEARING SYSTEM

Pressure waves pass through the auditory canal and vibrate the tympanic membrane (eardrum).

The ossicles transmit vibrations of the tympanic membrane to the oval window of the cochlea.

The cochlea contains a liquid. When it receives vibrations, the nerve endings send signals to the brain to be interpreted.

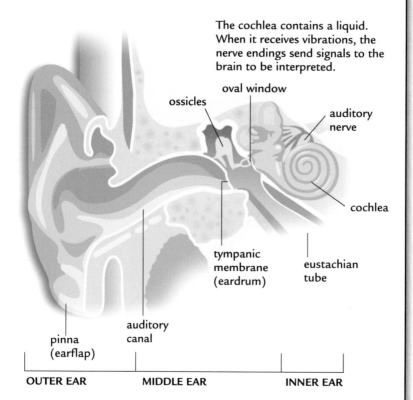

oval window

ossicles

auditory nerve

cochlea

tympanic membrane (eardrum)

eustachian tube

auditory canal

pinna (earflap)

OUTER EAR　　　　**MIDDLE EAR**　　　　**INNER EAR**

EAR TRUMPET

Go out in the street or a place where there are plenty of sounds to hear. Cup your hands behind your ears, and see how much more you can hear. Now make a funnel from rolled up paper, and leave a hole in the small end. Carefully put the small end to your ear. You should be able to hear even more now. Hearing aids in the 18th century (right) were similar to this. They were called ear trumpets.

DETECTING, LOCATING, AND IDENTIFYING SOUND

Hearing is an essential part of human communication. Without hearing it is not possible to detect speech or listen to music. Just as your two eyes produce a three-dimensional landscape of the world, so your two ears generate a kind of three-dimensional "soundscape." In this soundscape you can easily locate sounds, such as someone calling out your name.

Like the visual system, the auditory (or hearing) system has sense organs (the two ears), connections between the brain and the sense organs (the auditory nerves), and a part of the brain with the job of processing sounds from the ears (the auditory cortex).

The ear itself has three main parts: the outer ear, the middle ear, and the inner ear. The fleshy, outer part is called the pinna or auricle. It collects sounds and channels them down a curved pipe, called the auditory canal, toward a structure called the tympanic membrane (eardrum).

When sound waves enter the ear, they make the air move back and forth in the auditory canal, and that causes the eardrum to vibrate. Three small bones called the malleus (hammer), incus (anvil), and stapes (stirrup), which look a bit like the objects they are named for, are connected to the eardrum, and they vibrate as well. Their vibrations are carried through a tiny membrane called the oval window to the passage and structures of the inner ear. The most important part of the inner ear is a structure shaped like a snail shell called the cochlea, which is filled with fluid and has 15,000 sensitive hairs on its walls. As sound

HEARING AIDS

Modern hearing aids for deaf people are made up of tiny microphones and loudspeakers. They are positioned in the outer ear to increase the volume of sounds. Profoundly deaf people tend to have severe damage to the cochlea in their inner ear. Their hearing can be partially restored by embedding a type of hearing aid known as a cochlear implant inside their head (see below). Sounds are picked up by a microphone and carried to the speech receiver processor. It translates the sounds into electrical signals that then go to the transmitter and on to the implanted stimulator. The stimulator sends the signals to the auditory nerve, and the brain interprets the sounds.

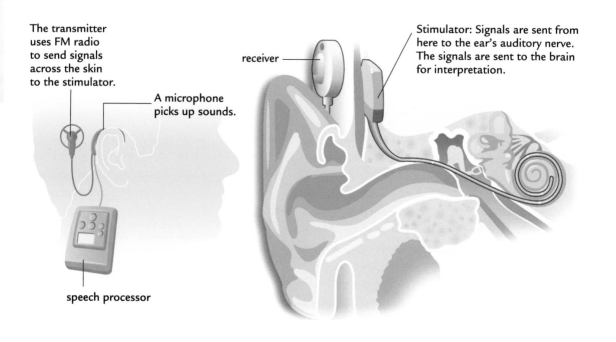

The transmitter uses FM radio to send signals across the skin to the stimulator.

receiver

Stimulator: Signals are sent from here to the ear's auditory nerve. The signals are sent to the brain for interpretation.

A microphone picks up sounds.

speech processor

vibrations travel from the oval window to the cochlea, they make the fluid move. The hairs detect the movement of the fluid and generate nerve impulses in the auditory nerve. The nerve carries the signals to the brain, which interprets them as recognizable sounds.

TOUCH, TASTE, AND SMELL

Touch, taste, and smell are other vital senses. Touch or feeling comes from sensitive nerve endings in the skin and from the hairs nearby. They respond to factors of pressure, pain, and

THE SMELL OF TASTE

Next time you eat a meal, try this experiment. Close off your nostrils just by holding your nose. Make sure you cannot smell. Now try tasting different types of foods. You may find they do not taste the same as usual. Smell plays a major part in how we taste things. If your nose is blocked when you have a cold, food seems tasteless.

temperature. Taste comes from taste buds, which are extremely sensitive bumps on the tongue (see below). Smell is detected by seven types of receptor cells inside the nose that are sensitive to roughly seven different types of smells. The receptor cells send signals down the olfactory (smell) nerves to parts of the brain that specialize in recognizing smells (see below).

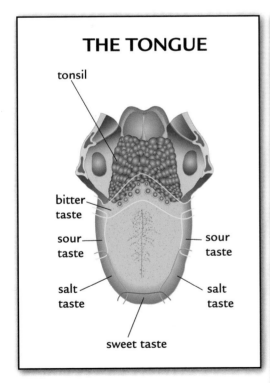

THE TONGUE

tonsil

bitter taste

sour taste

sour taste

salt taste

salt taste

sweet taste

Different areas of the tongue are most sensitive to one of four basic tastes: sweet, salt, sour, and bitter.

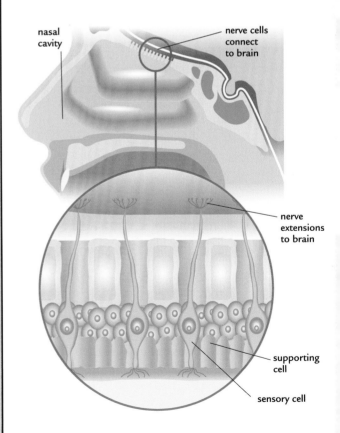

THE NASAL CAVITY

nasal cavity

nerve cells connect to brain

nerve extensions to brain

supporting cell

sensory cell

CHAPTER EIGHT

THE IMMUNE SYSTEM

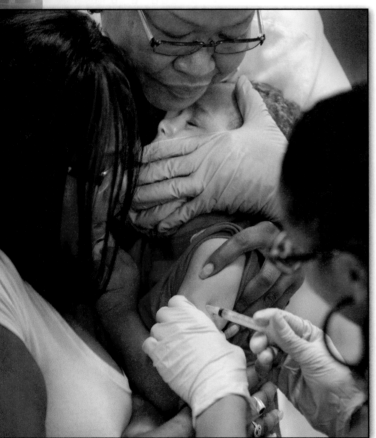

A health worker gives a vaccine containing inactive disease organisms to a child. More than 80 percent of U.S. children are vaccinated against certain diseases.

Usually it is only when something goes wrong with our body that we appreciate how important good health is.

Thankfully we have a complex group of cells and organs called the immune system that protects us from many diseases. We can also reduce the risk of illness by leading a healthy lifestyle.

Over the last 100 years or so the length of time people can generally expect to live (also called the life expectancy) and the effects of diseases have altered dramatically as lifestyles and environments have changed. At the start of the 20th century many people died before the age of 50. Many children died through infectious diseases such as measles. Today the average life expectancy in the United States is more than 75 years, and childhood deaths are relatively rare.

Improvements in diet, medicine, and hygiene during the 20th century played a

WHAT DO YOU EAT?

The typical U.S. diet contains too much fat, salt, and sugar. This kind of diet has been linked to the most common causes of death in the United States—cancer and heart disease. People are often unaware that they eat too much of certain food types, since food producers add extra ingredients to make them taste better. List all the foods you eat in one day. Check the package labels for sugar, fats (they may be called lipids), and salt (it may be called sodium). Most packages indicate the amount of each per 100g of the total contents. Find out whether you are eating more of each than you should.

crucial role in increasing life expectancy. Antibiotic medicines, which kill bacteria, and immunization programs reduced the number of deaths due to infectious disease. Today medicines that prepare the body for future infections called vaccines protect 80 percent of all children.

By contrast with a century ago, the major causes of death today in wealthy countries are cancer, heart disease, strokes, diabetes, and smoking-related diseases. Most of these illnesses stem from the way people live their lives. It is possible to reduce the risk of contracting many of the diseases that are caused by bad habits by altering diet, exercising

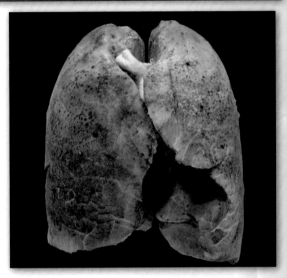

Black tar deposits in a lung, caused by smoking cigarettes.

SMOKING AND RELATED DISEASES

In many countries smoking is the main cause of death in people under the age of 65. Smoking causes lung cancer, and it can also increase the risk of developing other cancers, heart disease, and strokes. Tobacco smoke contains many substances, such as tar and carbon monoxide, that are poisonous to the body. Tar coats and irritates the linings of the lungs. Carbon monoxide attaches to red blood cells in place of oxygen. There are many other chemicals in cigarettes that cause cancer, too.

Why do you think people start smoking in the first place? Why do you think they continue to smoke, often for many years, despite the risks to their health?

THE INFLAMMATORY RESPONSE

▶ **A splinter bursts through the skin, bringing bacteria into the body. Damaged cells under the skin release a chemical called histamine. It moves into the bloodstream and alerts the immune system.**

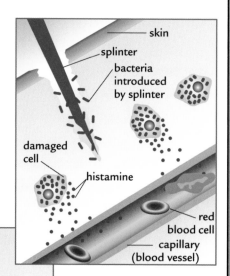

skin
splinter
bacteria introduced by splinter
damaged cell
histamine
red blood cell
capillary (blood vessel)

◀ **The histamine causes the capillary to become leaky and to expand a little. Complement proteins move from the blood toward the cells. These proteins attract white blood cells called phagocytes.**

bacteria
phagocyte
complement proteins

▶ **The phagocytes engulf and destroy the bacteria and the damaged cells. Then histamine release stops, and complement protein levels fall. Phagocytes are no longer attracted, and the tissue returns to normal.**

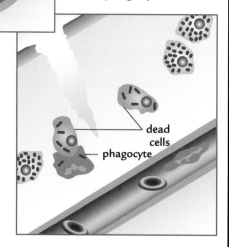

dead cells
phagocyte

more, and not smoking. Another major cause of death and disability today is traffic and other kinds of accidents.

THE BODY'S DEFENSES

Agents of disease such as bacteria and viruses that enter the body are called pathogens. People come into contact with pathogens, as well as chemical toxins, all the time. However, thanks to the work of the body's immune system, only very few of these harmful things succeed in making us ill.

There are three main lines of defense in the immune system. The first is the body's barriers—the skin and the membranes that cover entry points for pathogens, such as the eyes, nose, and mouth.

The second line of defense lies inside the body (see left). It involves mostly white blood cells called phagocytic cells, proteins called antibodies that attack pathogens, and a process known as the inflammatory

HOW DOES IMMUNIZATION WORK?

Most children in America are immunized against a number of diseases, such as diptheria, pertussis, and polio. During immunization a vaccine that contains a small amount of weakened or inactive disease organisms is introduced into your body. This is usually done by injection, although some vaccines are swallowed. The vaccine stimulates your immune system to produce antibodies. They are able to recognize and act against the disease organism.

Should you come into contact with the active form of the disease later in life, the antibodies will provide protection.

response. The first and second lines of defense are general ways of protecting the body against different kinds of pathogens. However, there is a third and final line of defense that is able to recognize, destroy, and remember specific pathogens even if they enter the body again years later.

REACTING TO INTRUDERS

The role the skin plays in the immune system is similar to that of an ancient city wall—it is a barrier against potential invaders. Unless the skin is pierced or damaged in some way, viruses or bacteria cannot normally penetrate it. Human skin also uses chemical weaponry to halt intruders. It produces acidic substances that make the skin hostile to many microorganisms.

Membranes line various parts of the body that are open to the air. Membranes inside the nose, for example, contain cells that produce a slimy substance called mucus. It traps microorganisms, and tiny hairlike filaments called cilia sweep the mucus and the microorganisms down into the throat to be swallowed. They then pass into the gut, where they are broken down.

Should a pathogen enter the body, through a cut, for example, it must deal with the second line of defense inside the body. The area around the infection becomes red and inflamed. This is the inflammatory response, in which the

A neutrophil surrounded by red blood cells. These important white blood cells are very mobile, moving swiftly through the blood to destroy pathogens.

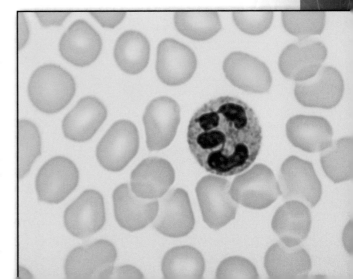

THE MMR JAB

Rather than using three injections, measles, mumps, and rubella are often immunized against all at once. This so-called MMR jab has been largely accepted in the United States, but its use remains controversial in Europe. Health authorities insist that the jab is safe.

Many members of the public, however, are convinced that the MMR jab can lead to psychological disorders such as autism. They accuse the health authorities of putting profit (since the single jab is cheaper than a course of three) before safety.

blood supply to the area increases. That enables white blood cells, which are attracted by chemical signals released from body tissues under attack, to reach the area as quickly as possible.

PHAGOCYTES

White blood cells called phagocytes are a key part of the second line of defense. They gobble up microorganisms and destroy them using strong chemicals. Phagocytes are produced in the bone marrow. There are several types of phagocytes. Neutrophils are the most common. They move to sites of infection, where they multiply and destroy bacteria and viruses. Their work done, the neutrophils die a few days later.

Neutrophils fight invaders with the help of a larger, longer-living, and much more powerful type of phagocyte called a macrophage. They are permanently present in many organs, where they constantly search for and destroy pathogens. Some float freely in the bloodstream and in lymph

The human lymphatic system is shown in blue; other important organs and vessels are shown in red.

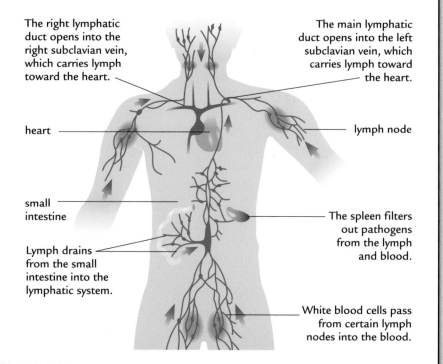

THE LYMPHATIC SYSTEM

The right lymphatic duct opens into the right subclavian vein, which carries lymph toward the heart.

The main lymphatic duct opens into the left subclavian vein, which carries lymph toward the heart.

heart

lymph node

small intestine

The spleen filters out pathogens from the lymph and blood.

Lymph drains from the small intestine into the lymphatic system.

White blood cells pass from certain lymph nodes into the blood.

(fluid that bathes the body's cells), look-ing for intruders. Macrophages also clean up dead neutrophils.

Another type of phagocyte, called an eosinophil, targets larger parasites such as disease-causing worms. Body cells that grow abnormally or are infected by viruses are killed by another important cell, the natural killer cell.

LYMPHOCYTES

The third and final line of defense centers around a type of white blood cell called a lymphocyte. Lymphocytes deal with most bacteria and viruses that enter the body. Like all white blood cells, lymphocytes develop in the bone marrow. However, unlike the others, lymphocytes are able to recognize and kill specific pathogens and then remember them in the future, allow-ing a swift and deadly response.

Some lymphocytes turn into cells called B cells, which are released straight into the bloodstream. During childhood other lymphocytes move through the bloodstream to the thymus, an organ in the chest. There they turn into cells called T cells.

B cells and T cells mostly occur in the lymphatic system. As in the circula-tory system, the lymphatic system has

A specific antibody attacks just one type of pathogen.

THE SPECIFIC NATURE OF ANTIBODIES

1. These are *a* antibodies.

2. The *a* antibodies attack *A* foreign particles and make them harmless.

3. These are *b* antibodies.

4. The *b* antibodies attack *B* foreign particles and make them harmless.

 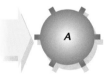

5. However, the *a* antibodies do not bind to proteins on foreign particle *B*, so they cannot attack it.

6. Similarly, the *b* antibodies do not bind to proteins on foreign particle *A*, so they cannot block it.

THE IMMUNE SYSTEM AND HIV

Some pathogens can trick the immune system. One of them is the HIV virus. This virus constantly alters the makeup of its outer surface, so phagocytes are unable to recognize it as a foreign body. The virus attacks white blood cells called helper T cells. It forces the helper T cell to make copies of its genes. That weakens the cell, which soon dies. With fewer and fewer helper T cells available, the immune system collapses. This disease is called AIDS.

vessels through which a liquid (lymph) flows. However, lymph is not pumped around the body by the heart as blood is. Lymph passes through the walls of capillaries, flows between the cells of organs, and is collected by a series of tiny lymph vessels. They carry the lymph back to the circulatory system along with the cells' waste products. The lymphatic system contains glands called nodes, where lymphocytes gather.

When they are needed, B cells turn into plasma cells. They in turn produce proteins called antibodies. Antibodies allow each specific B cell to detect and destroy a particular pathogen. Antibodies are Y-shaped proteins. Like a key fitting a lock, antibodies recognize and bind to proteins specific to the membranes of different pathogens. Plasma cells produce millions of antibodies at a time.

Unlike B cells, killer T cells attack body cells infected by a pathogen. Killer T cells recognize infected cells because they display proteins from the pathogen on their outer membranes once they have been infected. When it recognizes an infected cell, a killer T cell copies itself many times before attacking and destroying both cell and pathogen.

MAKING ANTIBODIES

Scientists have discovered how to boost immune systems by artificial means. In 1984 molecular biologists Cesar Milstein (born 1927) and Georges Köhler (1946–1995) won a Nobel Prize for inventing a technique to mass produce artificial antibodies. In 1998 these artificial (or monoclonal) antibodies were first used to treat breast cancer. Monoclonal antibodies are also used in pregnancy tests. They bind to a chemical that occurs inside pregnant women.

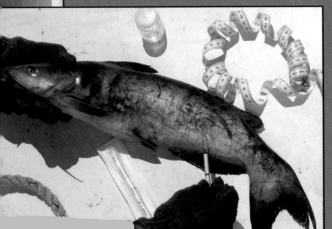

Blood drawn from this catfish will be used to develop monoclonal antibodies against infectious disease agents.

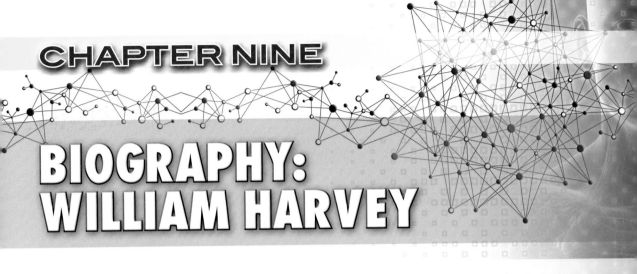

CHAPTER NINE

BIOGRAPHY: WILLIAM HARVEY

English physician William Harvey helped lay the foundations of modern medicine and physiology (how living organisms function). His work, based on direct observation and careful experiment, challenged long-held medical opinions and provided conclusive evidence that the heart acts as a pump, circulating blood throughout the body.

William Harvey was born on April 1, 1578, in Folkestone, Kent, southeast England, into a prosperous farming family. He was the eldest of seven sons, the only one to embark on a scientific career. His brothers became successful merchants in London.

When he was 10 years old William began his education at King's School, Canterbury. He won a scholarship to study medicine at Cambridge University, and entered Caius College in 1593, graduating in 1597. At the time, this was considered the best place in England to study medicine.

In 1599 William moved to the medical school at Padua University in Italy to study under the Italian Girolamo Fabrizio (1537–1619). He is usually known as Fabricius, the short Latin version of his name, or, in full, as Hieronymus Fabricius ab Aquapendente (Aquapendente is the town

William Harvey was an English physician who was the first to describe accurately and in detail the circulatory system and the properties of blood being pumped throughout the body by the heart.

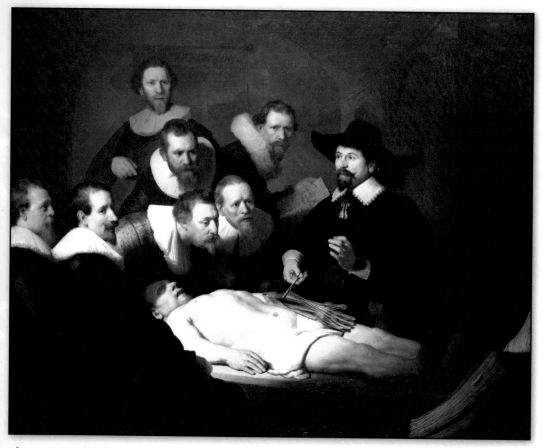

This painting by the Dutch painter Rembrandt (1601–1669) depicts a doctor instructing his students in anatomy. He is demonstrating the workings of the wrist and fingers.

in northern Italy where he was born). Fabricius specialized in the study of anatomy (the physical structure of animals and plants), and embryology (the study of embryos). The great astronomer and mathematician Galileo Galilei (1564–1642) was then professor of mathematics at Padua; his method of working out scientific laws from observation and experiment was attracting great attention. Harvey was strongly influenced by it, but probably never met Galileo.

PHYSICIAN TO THE KING AND COURT

Harvey obtained his medical degree in 1602 and returned to England, setting up in practice as a physician in London. He was very successful. His patients included Francis Bacon (1561–1626), lord chancellor of England, and the earl of Arundel, who became ambassador to the court of Ferdinand II (1578–1637), the Holy Roman emperor. Harvey was married in 1604 to

KEY DATES	
1578	Born on April 1
1588	Starts at King's School, Canterbury
1593	Enters Caius College, Cambridge University
1597	Graduates from Cambridge
1599	Enters the medical school of the University of Padua
1602	Graduates from Padua
1604	Marries Elizabeth Browne
1607	Elected a fellow of the Royal College of Physicians
1609	Appointed physician to St. Bartholomew's Hospital
1615–43	Professor at St. Bartholomew's
1616	Begins course of lectures on the heart and blood
1618–49	Serves as physician to King James I and then King Charles I
1628	Publishes work on circulation in *Anatomical Exercises on the Motion of the Heart and Blood in Animals*
1651	Publishes work on embryology
1657	Dies in London on June 3

Elizabeth Browne, daughter of the physician to King James I (1566–1625).

In 1607 Harvey was elected a "fellow" (member) of the Royal College of Physicians, and in 1609 was appointed physician to St. Bartholomew's Hospital. From 1615 to 1643 he taught there as a professor. It was traditional for a physician to give lectures attended by surgeons, and in 1616 Harvey began a course of lectures in which he explained his ideas and discoveries about the heart and blood.

Two years later he succeeded his father-in-law as physician to King James I and, after James's death he remained at court as physician to his son, King Charles I (1600–1649). Between 1629 and 1632 Harvey traveled widely, especially in Italy.

In 1642 civil war broke out in England between the supporters of Parliament and the supporters of King Charles I. Harvey may have been present with the king's army at the battle of Edgehill in October 1642. Many of his research papers were destroyed when the Parliamentary forces ransacked the king's palace at Whitehall. He was made warden of Merton College, Oxford in 1645 but lost his post after King Charles's defeat.

In 1654 Harvey was elected president of the Royal College of Physicians, but at 76 he felt was too old, so declined the honor. He died in London, on June 3, 1657. John Aubrey (1626–97), the English diarist, described Harvey's appearance: "In person he was not tall, but of the lowest stature; round faced, olivaster [olive-ish] complexion, little eyes, round, very black, full of spirits; his hair black as a raven, but quite white 20 years before he died."

STUDYING BLOOD CIRCULATION

Harvey was a highly successful physician, but his reputation rests on his medical research. While a student of Fabricius at Padua University, he

HEALING THE SICK

The origins of medical treatment in the West can be traced back to ancient Greece. Many philosophers attempted to understand the causes and treatment of disease. For example, the Greek physician Hippocrates of Cos (c. 460–377 or 359 BCE) tried to link environment and disease in his book *Airs, Waters, and Places.* His name lives on in the Hippocratic code—a set of laws that describes the way doctors should behave toward their patients. Many doctors still swear the Hippocratic oath today.

In Arab countries, the medical texts of ancient Greece and Rome were preserved and studied by Islamic scholars, while they were all but forgotten in the West for many centuries. The practice of medicine flourished, and hospitals and medical schools were established in cities across the Muslim empire from Baghdad in modern Iraq to Córdoba in Spain.

During the Middle Ages in Europe, the care of the sick was a religious duty undertaken by monks and nuns in infirmaries, special buildings attached to monasteries and convents.

In Paris, for example, the Hôtel Dieu (God's Hostel), an infirmary, was built onto the walls of Notre-Dâme cathedral. Such infirmaries often had herb gardens close by, where the medicinal plants needed for the treatment of patients were grown.

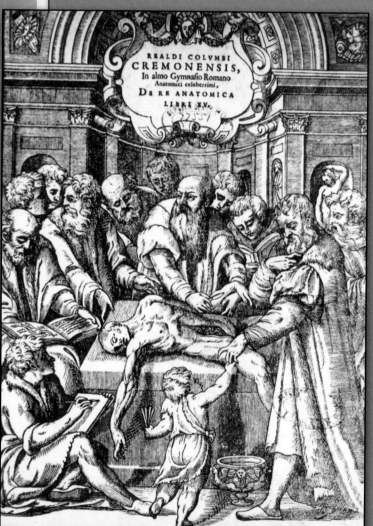

An anatomy class as shown in *On Anatomy* (1559) by Matteo Realdo Colombo (1516–1559), who was a professor at Padua University. The lecturer performed the dissection, while students consulted textbooks and took notes.

EARLY MEDICAL SCHOOLS

The first medical school in Europe was founded in Salerno, Italy (a part of the world where Arab influences were strong), between the 9th and 11th centuries. The Hospital of the Holy Ghost in Montpellier, France, founded in 1145, became an important training center for doctors. But as universities spread through western Europe, those studying medicine were often persuaded to give up practical studies in favor of university professorships. Medical teaching was firmly rooted in the ideas of Greek writers such as Aristotle and Galen.

By the end of the 15th century medical care was increasingly moving outside the control of the Church. In nearly every village, wise women made use of age-old herbal remedies to treat the sick. But institutions such as the College of Physicians, founded in London in 1518, grew up to regulate the practice of medicine and to ensure that only qualified people could dispense advice. Physicians had to pass an examination before being allowed to practice. Harvey undertook three oral examinations before obtaining his full license in 1604.

HOSPITALS

For the most part, hospitals were simply refuges where the chronically sick and poor were looked after until they died; little or no attempt was made to cure people. But gradually the habit developed of teaching students by practical lectures at the patient's bedside. Little by little hospitals became more professional places.

In 1607 Harvey became a fellow of the College of Physicians, entitling him to work at St. Bartholomew's. Founded in 1123 as London's first hospital, it had to take in every sick person judged to be curable. Harvey was obliged to see patients at least once a week in the great hall, and to prescribe treatment for them.

became interested in the way blood moves through the body. He came to realize that none of the exist-ing explanations was satisfactory.

The first person to describe blood in detail was Aristotle (384 BCE–322 BCE) in the 4th century bc. He thought that it was produced in the liver from food, carried through the body in the veins, and cooled by its passage through the brain. Two Greek physicians living in Alexandria, Egypt, developed these ideas. Herophilus (active 300–250 BCE) noted that arteries (large tubular vessels in the body) pulsate, or vibrate regularly. However, he failed to connect this with the beat of the heart. Erasistratus (c. 304–c. 250 BCE) thought that every organ in the body was served by veins, arteries, and nerves. He believed nerves were hollow and carried "nervous spirit," that arteries carried a kind of air called "animal spirit," and that veins carried blood from the heart.

GALEN'S HEART STUDIES

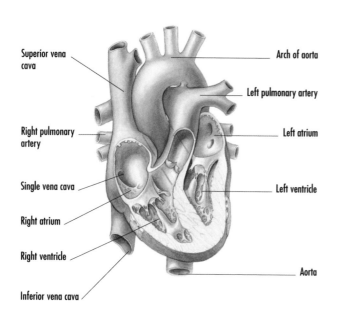

Galen observed that blood entered the right side of the heart through the vena cava (Latin for "hollow vein"). He knew that somehow blood had to move from the right side of the heart to the left side, and decided that it must do so by passing through tiny pores, or openings, in the "septum," the narrow wall separating the two sides of the heart (see left). On the left side, he believed, blood mixed with air entering the heart from the lungs. This mixture left the heart through the aorta (the largest artery) and was carried by other arteries through the body. The heart and arteries possessed a "pulsive power" that made them expand, drawing in blood from the tissues next to them as they did so. Galen thought some blood was carried to the head and the brain. There the blood absorbed "animal spirit," which produced consciousness. The animal spirit was carried through the hollow nerves to the muscles and sense organs.

Harvey discovered that blood enters the right side of the heart through the superior and inferior venae cavae (which converge into a single vena cava), then passes through the pulmonary arteries to the lungs, where it receives oxygen. It returns to the left atrium, passes into the left ventricle, and is pumped out through the aorta to the rest of the body, eventually returning to the right atrium.

Four centuries later Galen (c. 130–c. 201 CE), who lived at the height of the Roman empire, discovered that arteries carry blood, not air, and that nerves arise from the brain. He believed that blood was made in the liver, and from there it traveled through the veins to every part of the body, nourishing the organs and tissues.

Galen, who served as personal physician to the Roman emperor Marcus

The vivisection of a pig, as carried out by Galen and shown in a 1550 edition of his work. For many centuries the Greek physician was seen as an authority on anatomy, but Harvey disproved his theories on how the heart and blood worked.

Aurelius (121–180), was considered the foremost medical authority of his day. He obtained his ideas about anatomy through careful dissection (the cutting open of animals to learn more about their anatomy) and wrote more than 85 treatises on medical matters of all kinds. These remained the basis of all thinking about medicine and anatomy in Europe until the 16th century.

Matteo Realdo Colombo, professor of anatomy and surgery at Padua University, was one of the first to query Galen's teachings about blood. He did not think it traveled between the two sides of the heart through the walls of the septum as Galen said it did, and wondered if it flowed from the lungs to the heart, and perhaps also—by way of the pulmonary artery from the other side of the heart—back to the lungs. He saw that the heart alternately became bigger (dilated) and then smaller (contracted), and believed that it was the action of the heart as it contracted that pushed the blood into the lungs and out through the aorta.

UNDERSTANDING THROUGH DISSECTION

Colombo's ideas were not widely accepted (he appears to have been extremely quarrelsome) but Harvey certainly knew of them when he began his own investigations into the heart and blood. Like Galen, Harvey believed in using dissection. He examined the hearts and blood vessels of nearly 130 mammals and identified the valves (Harvey called them "clacks") that separate the atria and ventricles and allow blood to flow in one

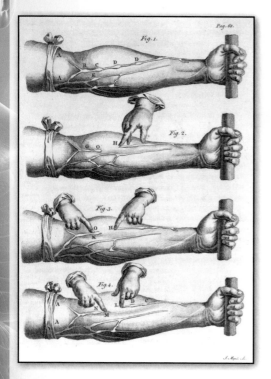

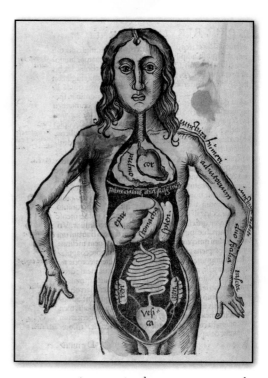

Harvey's proof (above) that blood returns to the heart through veins. The armband makes the veins stand out; the valves show as swellings. Because the valves within the veins only allow blood to flow one way, if pressure is put on a vein, blood will cease flowing toward the heart. A diagram (above right) from Reisch's *Pearls of Wisdom* (1508) gives a fairly realistic picture of the main human internal organs: heart, lungs, liver, spleen, and bladder.

direction only. He discovered that valves in the veins also allow blood to pass in only one direction—toward the heart.

The largest veins in the body are the superior and inferior venae cavae; these converge into a single vena cava as they enter the heart. Many of Harvey's experiments were carried out on live animals (this is called vivisection). When he tied the vena cava of a living snake he found that the vein bulged and the heart became smaller and paler in color. He concluded that blood must usually return to the heart through the vein, but he was blocking its path. When he tied the aorta, he found the heart swelled and became almost purple in color. The heart was swollen with blood; Harvey realized that the blood must usually leave the heart through the aorta, but he was preventing it doing so.

Harvey discovered that the ventricles of the heart are muscles that work as pumps, squeezing blood into the

HOW A CHICK GROWS INSIDE THE EGG

As well as his work on circulation, Harvey also conducted research into animal reproduction and the way embryos develop before birth (embryology). This was a subject about which little was known. Aristotle had suggested that the male seed produced the new animal; he thought the female's role was simply to nourish and protect the seed. Galen, on the other hand, believed that there were both male and female seeds, and that these united to produce the young animal.

Harvey's investigations led him to conclude that all animals develop from a female egg, even those that are born as live young, including human beings. This was a bold statement that was not definitely proved until the German-Estonian bio logist Karl Ernst von Baer (1792–1876), the founder of modern embryology, showed it to be true in 1827. Harvey's friends encouraged him to publish his researches into embryos in his book The Generation of Animals in 1651. His studies wereparticularly concerned with the growth of the chick inside the hen's egg. From his observations, made with the naked eye, he was able to describe accurately the order in which the parts of the body appear in the developing chick: the heart is the first organ to become visible and the feathers appear last. He was also able to show that chick embryos go through the same stages of development as the embryos of mammals such as deer.

The Generation of Animals was less influential than Harvey's book on blood circulation. Soon after his death scientists such as Marcello Malpighi and Robert Hooke (1635–1703) were using microscopes to make much more accurate observations than Harvey had been able to do. Harvey had speculated that male semen might contribute to the formation of the embryo. However, spermatozoa (sperm cells) are not visible to the naked eye. The first person to see them was the Dutch microscopist Antoni von Leeuwenhoek (1632–1723), using the powerful microscope he developed.

Anton van Leeuwenhoek was the first to accurately describe red blood cells, bacteria, and protozoa. He was also the first to see human sperm with the help of a powerful microscope of his own design.

pulmonary artery, which carries it to the lungs, and into the aorta, which carries it to all parts of the body. As Colombo thought, it is the contraction (the "systole") of the heart that causes the arteries to pulsate, not the dilation (the "diastole") of the heart as had previously been supposed. You can feel your own pulse as a regular throb on the inside of your wrist, close to where you wear your watch. Each beat registers a contraction of the heart.

Harvey calculated that with every beat an adult's heart pumps about 4 cubic inches (60 cm^3) of blood. This would mean the heart pumped about 68 gallons (259 liters) every hour, an amount of blood that would weigh more than 440 pounds (200 kg). It is clearly impossible for the body each hour to manufacture and consume a quantity of blood amounting to about three times the weight of the person. Harvey therefore concluded that a much smaller amount of blood circulates constantly through the body and is renewed and replenished as necessary.

In 1628 Harvey published his findings in a book called *Anatomical Exercises on the Motion of the Heart and Blood in Animals*. Galen was still very much admired and it was a brave man who dared to oppose his ideas. At first Harvey was scorned and ridiculed, and he was deserted by some of his patients. But by the time he died most doctors had come to accept his view of the circulation of the blood, and the influence of Galen soon declined.

Harvey accurately described almost every detail of the circulation of the blood. He observed that both arteries and veins divide repeatedly into ever smaller vessels, but he was unable to find the points where the arteries leading from the heart become veins, returning blood to the heart. Harvey did not have the use of a microscope. Four years after his death the Italian physiologist Marcello Malpighi (1628–1694), who did, was able to identify the network of delicate, thin-walled vessels called capillaries (from the Latin word for "hair") that connects the arteries and veins.

SCIENTIFIC BACKGROUND

Before 1590

Greek physician Galen (129–c. 199 AD) discovers that arteries carry blood, not air

Greek physician Herophilus (active 300–250) notes that arteries pulsate, but fails to connect this with the beating of the heart

Flemish anatomist Andreas Vesalius (1514–1564) publishes *On the Structure of the Human Body* (1543). It contains detailed descriptions of bones and the nervous system and disproves many of Galen's theories

1590

1600

1603 Hieronymus Fabricius (1537–1619), Italian anatomist and embryologist and teacher of Harvey, publishes *On the Valves in the Veins*

1609–1648 Harvey works as a physician at St. Bartholomew's Hospital in London

1610

1620 *New Organon* by English philosopher Francis Bacon (1561–1626) stresses the importance of experimentation in scientific work

1620

1621 Fabricius publishes work on embryology

1628 Harvey describes how blood circulates in his *Anatomical Exercises on the Motion of the Heart and Blood in Animals*

1630

1637 French philosopher Rene Descartes (1591–1650) publicizes Harvey's theories on the circulation of blood in his writings

1640

1650

1652 Danish physician Thomas Bartholin (1616–1680) describes the lymphatic system, defending Harvey's 1628 theory of blood circulation

1651 Harvey publishes his book on embryology, *The Generation of Animals*

1660

After 1660

1661 Using a microscope, Italian physiologist Marcello Malpighi (1628–1694) discovers blood capillaries

1665 English scientist Robert Hooke (1635–1703) publishes *Micrographia*, a collection of his observations using a microscope

1684 Dutch microscopist Anton van Leeuwenhoek (1632–1723) accurately describes red blood cells, bacteria and protozoa, and sperm cells

1827 German-Estonian embryologist Karl Ernst von Baer (1792–1876) describes the mammalian egg

POLITICAL AND CULTURAL BACKGROUND

1587 The Catholic Mary Queen of Scots (1542–1587) is executed on the orders of her cousin Queen Elizabeth I of England (1533–1603)

1593 The Irish rebel against English rule; the uprising lasts until 1601

1603–09 English playwright William Shakespeare (1564–1616) completes two of his greatest tragedies, *King Lear* and *Macbeth*

1608 French adventurer Samuel de Champlain (1567–1635) explores the North American coast and founds the city of Quebec in Canada

1619 The Dutch make Batavia (Indonesia) the center of their spice trade with the East Indies

1626 Governor Peter Minuit purchases the island of Manhattan from a local Native American tribe to found New Amsterdam (later New York)

1632 Dutch artist Rembrandt (1606–1669) completes the *Anatomy Lesson of Dr. Tulp,* which shows a body being dissected for medical research

1639 Japan's military governor Tokugawa Iemitsu (1604–1651) closes Japanese ports to foreigners in an effort to banish Christian missionaries

1648 The Thirty Years War, which has involved most countries in Europe, ends in the Peace of Westphalia

1649 The English Civil War ends with the beheading of King Charles I of Great Britain and Ireland (1600–1649) on January 30

1660 The monarchy is restored in Great Britain and Ireland as Charles I's son returns from Europe to be crowned King Charles II (1630–1685)

1665–66 The Great Plague strikes England, causing at least 70,000 deaths; the Great Fire of London that follows destroys many of the plague-carrying rats

alveolus Tiny air sac that forms bunches in the lungs through which exchange of oxygen and carbon dioxide takes place.

antibody Protein produced by white blood cells in response to an antigen; important in an immune response.

antigen Molecule (often on the surface of a foreign body) that the immune system can recognize.

aorta Major artery leading directly from the heart.

appendicular skeleton Part of the skeleton attached to the axial skeleton, including legs, pelvis, arms, and shoulders.

artery Branching vessels with elastic walls that carry blood from the heart around the body.

atrioventricular (AV) node Part of the heart that sends signals to slow down the SA node, allowing the contraction of the heart chambers to be regulated.

atrium One of a pair of heart chambers that receives blood before pumping it into a ventricle.

autonomic nervous system Part of the PNS that regulates the internal functions of the body automatically.

axial skeleton Part of the skeleton consisting of the skull, backbone, and rib cage.

bile A yellow fluid secreted by the liver; in the intestine it helps in the emulsification and absorption of fats.

Broca's area Part of the brain important for speech organization.

capillary Tiny, thin-walled blood vessels through which oxygen and nutrients pass into cells, with waste going the other way.

carbohydrates Sugar molecules important in respiration.

central nervous system (CNS) The brain and spinal cord and their supporting cells.

cochlea Coiled, fluid-filled structure in the inner ear that translates vibrations received at the tympanum into signals that go to the brain.

diffusion The movement of molecules of liquids and gases from points of high concentration to points of lower concentration.

digestion The breakdown by enzymes of food into small, easily absorbed molecules in the stomach.

emulsification The suspension of oil or fat droplets in water.

endocrine system System of glands that release hormones.

enzyme Protein that speeds up chemical reactions inside an organism.

exoskeleton Tough outer skin of animals such as insects, spiders, and crabs.

hemoglobin Pigment that occurs in red blood cells; binds to oxygen and carbon dioxide to carry these gases around the body.

hormone Chemical messenger that regulates life processes inside the body.

hypothalamus Part of the brain that releases chemicals that control the pituitary gland.

microvillus One of millions of hairlike structures that line the cells of the gut; they increase the surface area available for absorption.

nephron An excretory unit of the kidney.

neuron A nerve cell.

osteoporosis A condition leading to brittle and fragile bones that mainly affects older women.

pepsin Enzyme in the stomach that breaks down proteins into polypeptides.

peripheral nervous system (PNS) A network of nerves that spreads from the central nervous system to the rest of the body.

peristalsis Waves of muscular contraction that ripple along the walls of the digestive system to keep food moving.

pituitary gland Gland in the brain that releases hormones. They control the output of other endocrine glands.

platelet Tiny disk in the blood that helps clotting.

pleura One of a pair of delicate saclike membranes that wrap around the lungs.

red blood cell Cell that carries oxygen and carbon dioxide around the body.

respiration The liberation of energy from food using oxygen; occurs inside the cell.

retina Sensitive layer of cells at the back of the eye that is stimulated by light. It sends this visual information to the brain through the optic nerve.

saliva Liquid released by glands in the mouth. It helps lubricate food and also contains enzymes that begin the process of digestion.

sinoatrial (SA) node Part of the right atrium in the heart. Sends electrical impulses that regulate the heartbeat.

somatic nervous system Part of the PNS that gathers information from sensory organs and sends it to the central nervous system; also takes signals from the CNS to the muscles.

sphincter Ring of muscle that opens and closes entries to structures; found at the base of the stomach, for example.

tracheal system System of tubes used for breathing by most arthropods, such as insects.

tympanum Structure that receives sound vibrations in the air. Movements of the tympanum go to the cochlea after amplification by three inner ear bones and from the cochlea via nervous impulses to the brain.

vein Blood vessel that carries blood toward the heart from the capillaries.

vena cava Large vein that brings blood from the body into the heart.

ventricle One of a pair of heart chambers that receive blood from the atria. Blood from one is pumped to the lungs; blood from the other leaves via the aorta to move through the body.

vitamin An organic (carbon-containing) substance essential in tiny amounts for nutrition.

Wernicke's area Part of the brain important for interpreting language.

white blood cell Colorless blood cell that forms part of the immune system.

American Association of Anatomists
(AAA)
9650 Rockville Pike
Bethesda, MD 20814-3998
(301) 634-7910
Web site: http://www.anatomy.org
AAA is dedicated to the advancement of
anatomical science through
research, education, and professional
development. AAA is the professional home for the anatomical
sciences community.

Anatomical Society
c/o Department of Anatomy and Human
Sciences
King's College London
Room 5.9N Hodgkin Building (Guy's
Campus)
London, England SE1 1UL
Tel: +44 (0)207 848 8234
Web site: http://www.anatsoc.org.uk
The Anatomical Society's aims are to
promote, develop, and advance
research and education in all aspects
of anatomical science. It achieves
these aims by organizing scientific
meetings; publishing the *Journal of
Anatomy and Aging Cell*; and mak-
ing annual awards of Ph.D.
studentships, grants, and prizes.

Biology Editorial Office
MDPI
Postfach, CH-4005
Basel, Switzerland
Tel.: +41 61 683 77 34
Web site: http://www.mdpi.com/journal/
biology

Biology is an international, peer-
reviewed, open access journal of
biological science, published by
MDPI online quarterly.

The Biology Project
Dept. of Biochemistry and Molecular
Biophysics
College of Science
The University of Arizona
P.O. Box 210041
1306 East University Boulevard
Tucson, AZ 85721-0041
(520) 621-6354
Web site: http://www.biology.arizona.edu
The Biology Project delivers student-
oriented, highly interactive
biology-centered learning materials
online. These learning materials are
used to support biology lecture, lab-
oratory, and discussion sessions of
general education courses. The
Biology Project is fun, richly illus-
trated, and tested on thousands of
students. It has been designed for
biology students specifically who
will benefit from the real-life appli-
cations of biology and the inclusion
of up-to-date research findings.

Centers for Disease Control and
Prevention (CDC)
1600 Clifton Road
Atlanta, GA 30333
800-CDC-INFO (800-232-4636)
Web site: http://www.cdc.gov
The CDC's mission is to create the
expertise, information, and tools that
people and communities need to

protect their health – through health promotion, prevention of disease, injury and disability, and preparedness for new health threats. The CDC seeks to accomplish its mission by working with partners throughout the nation and the world to monitor health, detect and investigate health problems, conduct research to enhance prevention, develop and advocate sound public health policies, implement prevention strategies, promote healthy behaviors, foster safe and healthful environments, and provide leadership and training.

Khan Academy
P.O. Box 1630
Mountain View, CA 94042
Web site: http://www.khanacademy.org/science/biology
Khan Academy is a not-for-profit educational organization whose mission is to provide a free, world-class education to anyone, anywhere. It has an entire section devoted to biology, including evolution and natural selection, cells and cell division, heredity and genetics, cellular respiration, the tree of life, photosynthesis, human biology, and immunology. Its other online materials cover subjects ranging from math and finance to history and art. With thousands of bite-sized videos, step-by-step problems, and instant data, Khan Academy provides a rich and engaging learning experience.

National Institutes of Health (NIH)
9000 Rockville Pike
Bethesda, MD 20892
Web site: http://www.nih.gov
NIH's mission is to seek fundamental knowledge about the nature and behavior of living systems and the application of that knowledge to enhance health, lengthen life, and reduce the burdens of illness and disability.

National Science Foundation
Directorate for Biological Sciences
4201 Wilson Boulevard
Arlington, VA 22230
(703) 292-5111
Web site: http://www.nsf.gov/dir/index.jsp?org=BIO
The mission of the Directorate for Biological Sciences (BIO) is to enable discoveries for understanding life. BIO-supported research advances the frontiers of biological knowledge, increases our understanding of complex systems, and provides a theoretical basis for original research in many other scientific disciplines. The Directorate for Biological Sciences supports research to advance understanding of the principles and mechanisms governing life. Research studies extend across systems that encompass biological molecules, cells, tissues, organs, organisms, populations, communities, and ecosystems up to and including the global biosphere.

Science Olympiad
2 Trans Am Plaza Drive, Suite 415
Oakbrook Terrace, IL 60181
(630) 792-1251
Web site: http://www.soinc.org
Science Olympiad is a national non-
profit organization dedicated to
improving the quality of K–12 science
education, increasing male, female,
and minority interest in science, cre-
ating a technologically literate
workforce, and providing recognition
for outstanding achievement by both
students and teachers. These goals
are achieved by participating in
Science Olympiad tournaments and
non-competitive events, incorporat-
ing Science Olympiad into classroom
curriculum, and attending teacher
training institutes.

WEB SITES

Due to the changing nature of Internet
links, Rosen Publishing has developed
an online list of Web sites related to the
subject of this book. This site is updated
regularly. Please use this link to access
the list:

http://www.rosenlinks.com/CORE/Body

Chiras, Daniel D. *Human Body Systems*. Burlington, MA: Jones & Bartlett Learning, 2012.

Cohen, Barbara Janson. *Memmler's Structure and Function of the Human Body*. Philadelphia, PA: Lippincott Williams & Wilkins, 2012.

Distefano, Matthew. *Homework Helpers: Biology*. Pompton Plains, NJ: Career Press, 2011.

DK Publishing. *Human Body: A Visual Encyclopedia*. New York, NY: DK Publishing, 2012.

Hoefnagels, Mariëlle. *Biology: The Essentials*. New York, NY: McGraw-Hill Science/Engineering/Math, 2012.

Kratz, René Fester, and Donna Rae Siegfried. *Biology for Dummies*. Hobooken, NJ: For Dummies, 2010.

Mader, Sylvia. *The Concepts of Biology*. New York, NY: McGraw-Hill Science/Engineering/Math, 2010.

Mader, Sylvia, and Michael Windelspecht. *Human Biology*. New York, NY: McGraw-Hill Science/Engineering/Math, 2011.

Parker, Steve. *The Human Body Book*. New York, NY: DK Adult, 2013.

Reece, Jane B., et al. *Campbell Biology*. 9th ed. New York, NY: Benjamin Cummings, 2010.

Reece, Jane B., et al. *Study Guide for Campbell Biology*. New York, NY: Benjamin Cummings, 2010.

Roberts, Alice. *The Complete Human Body*. New York, NY: DK Publishing, 2010.

Shubin, Neil. *Your Inner Fish: A Journey into the 3.5-Billion-Year History of the Human Body*. New York, NY: Vintage, 2009.

Thibodeau, Gary A., and Kevin T. Patton. *The Human Body in Health & Disease*. St. Louis, MO: Mosby, 2009.

Tortora, Gerard J., and Bryan H. Derrickson. *Introduction to the Human Body*. Hoboken, NJ: Wiley, 2009.

Walker, Richard. *Human Body*. New York, NY: DK Children, 2009.

Wilhelm, Patricia Brady. *A Brief Atlas of the Human Body*. New York, NY: Benjamin Cummings, 2010.

PHOTO CREDITS